Greetings *California!*

It takes you there!

HSP CALIFORNIA EXCURSIONS

Sea of Stars

Senior Authors

Isabel L. Beck • Roger C. Farr • Dorothy S. Strickland

Authors

Alma Flor Ada • Roxanne F. Hudson • Margaret G. McKeown
Robin C. Scarcella • Julie A. Washington

Harcourt
SCHOOL PUBLISHERS

www.harcourtschool.com

Sea of Stars

Harcourt

SCHOOL PUBLISHERS

www.harcourtschool.com

Theme 4
Dream Big

Contents

Comprehension Strategies 10
Theme 4 Opener 14

Lesson 16

⭐ **Language Arts**

🌀 *Focus Skill* Setting 18

Vocabulary 20

Mr. Putter and Tabby Write the Book...22
by Cynthia Rylant • illustrated by Arthur Howard • REALISTIC FICTION

Interview with Author Pam Muñoz Ryan........ 44
INTERVIEW

Paired Selections

🌐 **Social Studies**

Connections 46

Theme Writing

Reading-Writing Connection 48
Student Writing Model: Story

🌐 **Social Studies**   **Lesson 17**

🌀 *Focus Skill* Setting 54

Vocabulary 56

Annie's Gifts 58
by Angela Shelf Medearis • illustrated by Anna Rich • REALISTIC FICTION

Sarah Enters a Painting 88
by Susan Katz • illustrated by R.W. Alley • POETRY

Paired Selections

🎨 **Art**

Connections 90

 Music

Lesson 18

Words with *oi* and *oy*..................................94

Vocabulary 96

Ah, Music! 98
by Aliki • Nonfiction

 Language Arts

Come, My Little Children, Here Are Songs For You..................................112
by Robert Louis Stevenson • illustrated by Vladimir Radunsky • Poetry

Paired Selections

Connections 114

 Social Studies

Lesson 19

Locate Information 118

Vocabulary 120

The Life of George Washington Carver..................................122
by Joli K. Stevens • Biography

Paired Selections

Science

Nutty Facts About Peanuts 136
by Gail Skroback Hennessey • from *Ranger Rick* • Magazine Article

Social Studies

Connections 138

Lesson 20 **Theme Review**

READERS' THEATER

What's My Job?..................................142
Game Show

COMPREHENSION STRATEGIES

North America..................................154
Social Studies Textbook

Social Studies

Theme 5
Better Together

Contents

Theme 5 Opener 158

Social Studies Lesson 21

Plot 162

Vocabulary 164

A Chair for My Mother 166
by Vera B. Williams • REALISTIC FICTION

Saving Money 192
by Mary Firestone • NONFICTION

Paired Selections

Social Studies

Connections 196

Theme Writing   Reading-Writing Connection 198
Student Writing Model: Description

Social Studies Lesson 22

Plot 204

Vocabulary 206

Serious Farm 208
by Tim Egan • FANTASY

Beyond Old MacDonald 234
by Charley Hoce • illustrated by Eugenie Fernandes • POETRY

Paired Selections

Language Arts

Connections 236

Science

Lesson 23

Words with *oo, ew, ue, ui, ou* 240

Vocabulary 242

The Bee 244
by Sabrina Crewe • NONFICTION

Paired Selections

California Bee Business 274
by Dimarie Santiago • NONFICTION

Science

Connections 276

Science

Lesson 24

Use Graphic Aids 280

Vocabulary 282

Watching in the Wild 284
by Charnan Simon • from *Click* • NONFICTION

Paired Selections

Chimp Computer Whiz 298
from *Ask* • MAGAZINE ARTICLE

Science

Connections 300

 Social Studies

Lesson 25 **Theme Review**

READERS' THEATER

Town Hall 304
INTERVIEW

COMPREHENSION STRATEGIES

A Time For Patience 316
from *Fables from Aesop* • retold and illustrated by Tom Lynch • FABLE

Language Arts

Theme 6
Seek and Find

Contents

Theme 6 Opener 320

Social Studies   Lesson 26

Cause and Effect.. 324

Vocabulary 326

Where on Earth Is My Bagel? 328
by Frances and Ginger Park • illustrated by Grace Lin • FICTION

Paired Selections

South Korea 354
by Susan E. Haberle • NONFICTION

Social Studies

Connections 356

Theme Writing   Reading-Writing Connection 358
Student Writing Model: Research Report

Social Studies   Lesson 27

Cause and Effect 364

Vocabulary 366

My Name is Gabriela 368
by Monica Brown • illustrated by John Parra • BIOGRAPHY

Paired Selections

Gabriela Mistral: A Poet's Life in Photos 386
by Alma Flor Ada and F. Isabel Campoy • PHOTO ESSAY

Social Studies

Connections 390

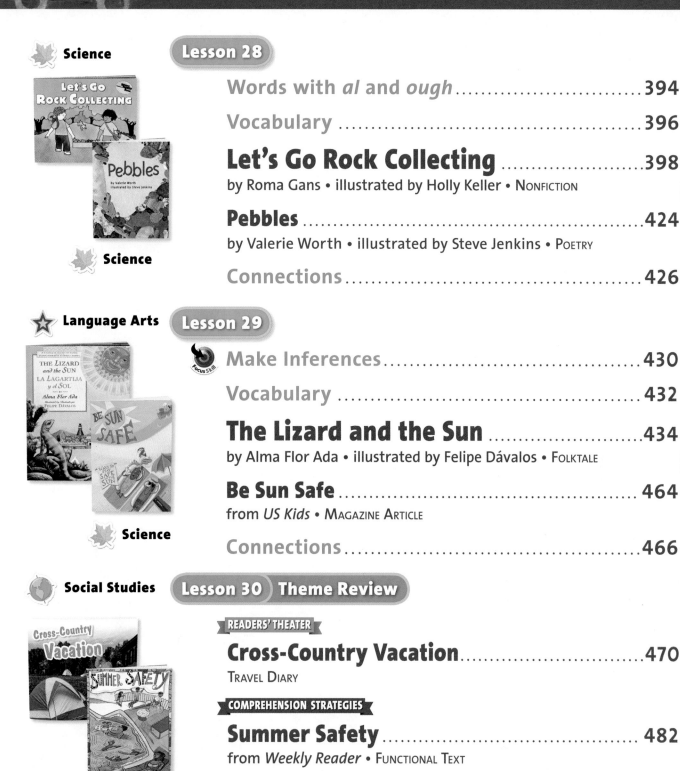

Science

Lesson 28

Words with *al* and *ough* 394

Vocabulary 396

Let's Go Rock Collecting 398
by Roma Gans • illustrated by Holly Keller • NONFICTION

Pebbles 424
by Valerie Worth • illustrated by Steve Jenkins • POETRY

Paired Selections

Science

Connections 426

Language Arts

Lesson 29

Make Inferences 430

Vocabulary 432

The Lizard and the Sun 434
by Alma Flor Ada • illustrated by Felipe Dávalos • FOLKTALE

Be Sun Safe 464
from *US Kids* • MAGAZINE ARTICLE

Paired Selections

Science

Connections 466

Social Studies

Lesson 30 **Theme Review**

READERS' THEATER

Cross-Country Vacation 470
TRAVEL DIARY

COMPREHENSION STRATEGIES

Summer Safety 482
from *Weekly Reader* • FUNCTIONAL TEXT

Social Studies

Comprehension Strategies

Before You Read

Think about what you already know.
Look over the words and pictures before you read.

Set a purpose.
Decide why you are reading.

I want to enjoy reading a story.

While You Read

Use story structure.

Think about a story's characters, setting, and plot.

Use graphic organizers.

Use a story map, web, or chart to help you read.

Monitor your reading.

Use fix-up strategies such as reading ahead or rereading.

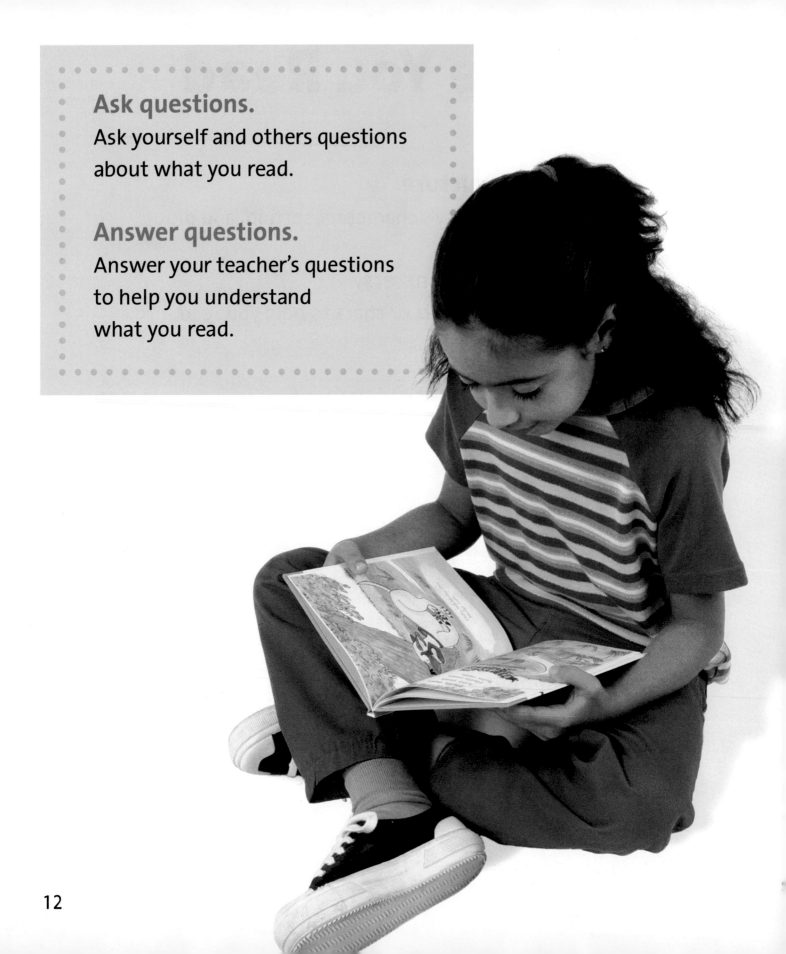

Ask questions.
Ask yourself and others questions about what you read.

Answer questions.
Answer your teacher's questions to help you understand what you read.

After You Read

Summarize.

Think about the main ideas of what you read.

Make Connections.

Think about how what you read is like something else.

READING-WRITING
CONNECTION

	Lesson 16 >	Lesson 17 >
Selection Titles	**Mr. Putter and Tabby Write the Book** Interview with Author Pam Muñoz Ryan	**Annie's Gifts** Sarah Enters a Painting
Comprehension Strategies	Monitor Comprehension: Read Ahead	Monitor Comprehension: Read Ahead
Focus Skills	Setting	Setting

CALIFORNIA STANDARDS
ENGLISH-LANGUAGE ARTS STANDARDS

Theme (4) Dream Big

▶ *Music,* Xavier Cortada

Lesson 18 ▶

Ah, Music!
Come, My Little Children, Here Are Songs for You
Answer Questions

Words with *oi* and *oy*

Reading 1.1 Recognize and use knowledge of spelling patterns (e.g., diphthongs, special vowel spellings) when reading.

Lesson 19 ▶

The Life of George Washington Carver
Nutty Facts About Peanuts
Answer Questions

Locate Information

Reading 2.1 Use titles, tables of contents, and chapter headings to locate information in expository text.

Lesson 20 **Review**

What's My Job?
North America

Review Skills and Strategies

Reading 1.1 Recognize and use knowledge of spelling patterns (e.g., diphthongs, special vowel spellings) when reading; Reading 2.1 Use titles, tables of contents, and chapter headings to locate information in expository text.

Contents

Setting 18

Learn to identify when and where a story takes place.

Vocabulary 20

Read, write, and learn the meanings of new words.

Mr. Putter and Tabby Write the Book by Cynthia Rylant
illustrated by Arthur Howard 22

- Learn the features of realistic fiction.

- Read ahead to learn more about the story.

Interview with California Author Pam Muñoz Ryan 44

Read an interview with a children's book author.

Connections 46

- Compare texts.

- Review phonics skills.

- Reread for fluency.

- Write about a setting.

Realistic Fiction

CYNTHIA RYLANT

Mr. Putter & Tabby
Write the Book

Illustrated by
Arthur Howard

Interview
with Author Pam Muñoz Ryan

Interview

17

Focus Skill

 **Setting**

Every story has characters, a setting, and a plot. The **setting** is when and where the story takes place.

Read this story beginning. Look for words that tell about the setting.

In the winter, Daniel and his dog, Duke, liked to play in the backyard.

The words *in the winter* tell when. The words *in the backyard* tell where.

Setting	
When	Where
in the winter	in the backyard

Read this story. Look for clue words that tell when the story takes place.

Mia's Snowman

It was Saturday, and Mia had made a snowman near the barn on her family's farm. It had taken her most of the day to build him.

Now it was time for dinner, and she had one more thing to add. Mia reached into her pocket and pulled out a scarf. "Now you won't get cold tonight," she said.

Setting	
When	Where
• Saturday	•
•	•
•	

 www.harcourtschool.com/reading

Try This!

Look back at the story above. What words tell where the story happens?

19

Vocabulary

enchanting

cozy

instead

thrilled

review

celebrate

How to Be a Poet

I like the way a poem makes a picture with words. That's why I want to write a poem of my own. I want it to sound **enchanting** when I read it to my parents. Now I have to think of something to write about.

I'll settle into a soft, **cozy** chair near a window. I'll look out at my snowy backyard. I might see a rabbit hopping across the snow. I'll write a word picture of what I see.

When I look out, I see my dog, Lulu, **instead** of a rabbit. She's playing in the snow. I grab my pencil and write as fast as I can.

My parents are **thrilled** with my poem. They clap and tell me they can see the picture I made with words. That's the best **review** I could ask for! They even want to **celebrate** by taking me skating. I'm going to like being a poet!

 www.harcourtschool.com/reading

Word Detective

 Where else can you find the Vocabulary Words? Look in your favorite magazine. Listen for the words on your favorite TV show. When you see or hear one of the words, write it in your vocabulary journal and tell where you found it. Happy word hunting!

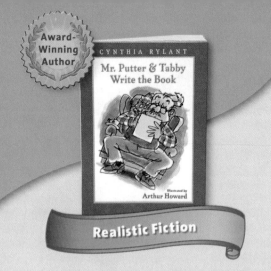

CYNTHIA RYLANT

Mr. Putter & Tabby
Write the Book

Illustrated by
Arthur Howard

Realistic Fiction

Genre Study

Realistic fiction is a story that could really happen. Look for

- characters who do things that real people do.

- a realistic setting.

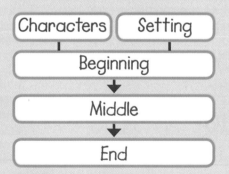

| Characters | Setting |
| Beginning |
| Middle |
| End |

Comprehension Strategy

Monitor comprehension—Read ahead if you do not understand something.

22

Mr. Putter and Tabby Write the Book

by CYNTHIA RYLANT

illustrated by ARTHUR HOWARD

24

1
An Idea

In the winter a big snow always came to Mr. Putter's house. Mr. Putter and his fine cat, Tabby, liked big snows. But they couldn't go out in them. They were too old. Mr. Putter might slip and break something. Tabby might catch a bad cold.

They didn't mind staying in, though, because Mr. Putter's house was so cozy. It had nice soft chairs. It had velvet pillows. It had a fireplace. Staying in was all right when everything was so soft and velvety and warm.

One day when Mr. Putter and Tabby were inside for a big snow, Mr. Putter got an idea. His idea was to write a book.

He had everything a writer needed:
a soft chair, a warm fire, and a good cat.
And he had a pen and plenty of paper.

"I have always wanted to write a mystery
novel," Mr. Putter said to Tabby.

So he brought out lots of paper,
lit the fire, plumped his chair, and
got ready to begin.

First he had to think of a title.
He thought and thought
and thought.

Finally he told Tabby, "I shall call my book *The Mystery of Lighthouse Cove*."

It was a very good title. It was full of mystery. As a boy he had read lots of books with titles like that.

Mr. Putter was so pleased, he decided
to fix a snack. He went into the kitchen
and fixed a big apple salad, a pan of corn
muffins, some custard pudding, and a
cheese ball.

Mr. Putter spent three minutes on his title and four hours on his snack.

Then he took a nap. Mystery writing was not easy work.

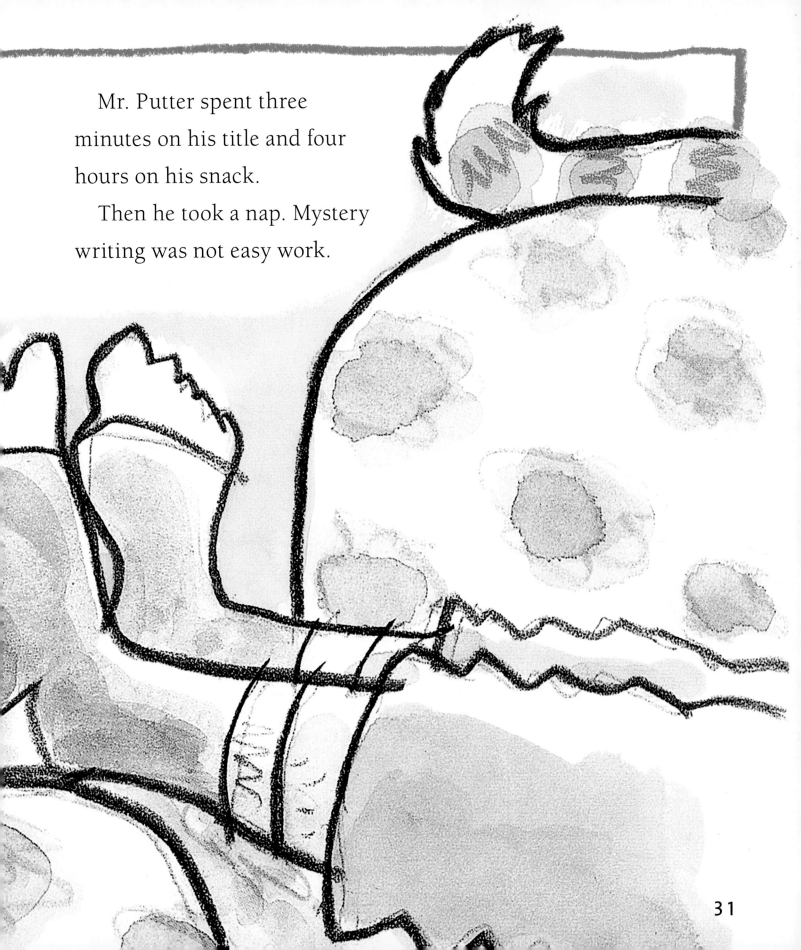

2

Chapter One

On the second day that he was a mystery writer, Mr. Putter had a nice long breakfast with Tabby of oatmeal and tea. Then he settled down to write again. But first he had to stoke the fire.

Then he had to clean Tabby's ears.

Then he had to find a sweater.

Then he had to move his
chair closer to the window.
Then he had to move it back.

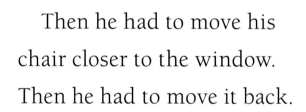

Then he settled down again.
He was ready to write. Mr.
Putter looked at the walls and
he thought. He thought and
thought and thought.

Finally he wrote: CHAPTER ONE.

He began to think some more. As he
was thinking, he looked out the window.

He decided to fix a snack. He went into the kitchen and fixed twenty boiled eggs and a vegetable stew. Mr. Putter spent one minute on CHAPTER ONE and three hours on eggs and stew.

Then he took a bath. Then he took a nap. Mystery writing wore him out.

3
Good Things

The third day that he was a
mystery writer, Mr. Putter woke
up ready to write again. He liked
being a writer ready to write.

First he and Tabby had cinnamon toast and tea. Then Mr. Putter petted Tabby and began to think. He looked out of his window, thinking. He looked at his fire, thinking. He looked at Tabby, thinking.

GOOD THINGS
Yellow cats
Old sweaters
Cinnamon toast
Long baths
Good dogs
Rain

Mr. Putter thought how blue the sky was. He thought how warm the fire felt. He thought how nice it was to be with Tabby. He thought about so many good things that he began to write them down. He wrote and wrote and wrote. Mr. Putter wrote all day long.

When he finally stopped writing, the big snow had melted. Mr. Putter went next door with Tabby to visit Mrs. Teaberry and her good dog, Zeke. They had some french-fried butternut squash for supper.

Then Mr. Putter read *Good Things*. When he finished, Mrs. Teaberry said it was "enchanting." She said Mr. Putter was a wonderful writer. She said she could listen forever.

"I wanted to write *The Mystery of Lighthouse Cove*," Mr. Putter said sadly. "But I wrote *Good Things* instead. And I ate too much and took too many naps."

Mrs. Teaberry told him not to worry. She said the world is full of mystery writers. But writers of good things are few and far between.

Mr. Putter did not feel so sad then. He did not feel sad at all. In fact, he was thrilled. (Every writer loves a good review.)

To celebrate good reviews and good neighbors, Mr. Putter took Mrs. Teaberry and Tabby and Zeke out for vanilla malts.

And Mr. Putter had so much fun and thought of so many good things that he could not wait for the next big snow . . .

. . . so he could be a writer again.

Think Critically

R2.5
R3.1
W1.1

1 How is the setting of this story different from the setting in "Big Bushy Mustache"?

 SETTING

2 Why does Mr. Putter keep doing other things instead of writing his book?

DRAW CONCLUSIONS

3 Why does Mr. Putter begin making a list of good things? IMPORTANT DETAILS

4 Why does the author repeat the words *he thought* so many times in the story?

AUTHOR'S CRAFT/WORD CHOICE

5 **WRITE** What good things do you think Mr. Putter will write about next time? Use details from the story to support your answer. SHORT RESPONSE

CALIFORNIA STANDARDS
ENGLISH-LANGUAGE ARTS STANDARDS—Reading 2.5 Restate facts and details in the text to clarify and organize ideas; **Reading 3.1** Compare and contrast plots, settings, and characters presented by different authors; **Writing 1.1** Group related ideas and maintain a consistent focus.

Meet the Author
Cynthia Rylant

Cynthia Rylant has written many books about Mr. Putter and his cat, Tabby. How does she get her ideas? She says, "I move furniture. I eat cookies. I move more furniture." That sounds a lot like Mr. Putter!

Meet the Illustrator
Arthur Howard

Arthur Howard has been drawing all his life. For seven years, he acted in a children's television show. Then he decided to go back to his first love, drawing pictures.

 www.harcourtschool.com/reading

43

Interview

Interview with CALIFORNIA Author
Pam Muñoz Ryan

Many children who read "Mr. Putter and Tabby Write the Book" want to know more about being a writer. Our interviewer spoke with California author Pam Muñoz Ryan to find out more.

Interviewer: What kind of books do you like to write?

Muñoz Ryan: I like to write both picture books and chapter books. They are different from each other. When I write a picture book, I use fewer words because the illustrator tells part of the story with pictures. When I write a chapter book, I describe with more details. I try to make a picture in the reader's mind with my words.

Interviewer: Where do you get the ideas for your books?

Muñoz Ryan: A story doesn't always come from one idea. For me, a story comes from many ideas that are joined together. Ideas are everywhere.

Interviewer: Is there anything else you would like children to know about being a writer?

Muñoz Ryan: Before one of my stories becomes a book, I have rewritten it many times. Sometimes I rewrite it more than twenty times! Writing is like many other things. The harder you work and the more you practice, the better you become.

Interviewer: Thank you for talking with me.

Muñoz Ryan: You're welcome. Happy writing!

Pam
Muñoz
Ryan

45

Connections

Comparing Texts

1. Think about the story of Mr. Putter and the interview with Pam Muñoz Ryan. How are they alike? How are they different?

2. What kinds of writing have you tried?

3. How can writers share their work?

Phonics
R1.1

Make a Chart

Write _knee_, _write_, _cough_, and _graph_ in a chart.
Below each word, write two more words that have the same spelling and sound as the underlined letters.
Read your words to a partner.

knee	write	cough	graph
know			

CALIFORNIA STANDARDS
ENGLISH-LANGUAGE ARTS STANDARDS—Reading 1.1 Recognize and use knowledge of spelling patterns (e.g., diphthongs, special vowel spellings) when reading; **Reading 1.6** Read aloud fluently and accurately and with appropriate intonation and expression; **Reading 3.1** Compare and contrast plots, settings, and characters presented by different authors; **Writing 1.1** Group related ideas and maintain a consistent focus.

Fluency Practice
R1.6

Read with Feeling

Read the story again with a partner. Take turns reading one or two pages at a time. Make your voices go up and down to show how Mr. Putter is feeling.

Writing
W1.1

Setting

Mr. Putter likes to write in his house during the winter. When and where do you like to write? Describe the setting. Use a setting chart to help you.

My Writing Checklist

Writing Trait ➤ Organization

✔ I use a setting chart to plan my writing.

✔ I tell when and where I write.

Setting	
When	Where

Reading-Writing Connection

Story

A good **story** has strong characters, an interesting beginning, and a good ending. I wrote this story after I read "Mr. Putter and Tabby Write the Book."

The Shiny Red Pencil
by Dashell

Lipton's friend Greg came over to play ball.
"I can't play," Lipton said. "My report is due tomorrow, but I don't know how to get started!"

Greg said Lipton could use his special red pencil. It would help him write.

Lipton tried it. Once he started, he couldn't stop!

Finally, Greg said, "I've got a special pencil that will help you stop."

Lipton looked up. "Where is it?"

Greg quickly slid the shiny red pencil out of Lipton's hand. "Right here!" he said. Lipton laughed. Then both boys ran out to play ball.

Writing Trait

ORGANIZATION A story has real or make-believe characters and a setting. It also has a beginning, middle, and end.

Writing Trait

WORD CHOICE I use colorful words to help make my writing interesting.

Here's how I write a story.

1. I look back at other stories I have read. I think about what happened and how the characters acted. I also think about things that have happened to me.

2. I brainstorm story ideas. I make a list or use a web.

> ○
>
> Mall walk with Dad
> Bike trip to park
> Math game at Ellen's house
> A special writing pencil

3. I choose one idea for writing. I circle the idea I think will be most interesting to my readers.

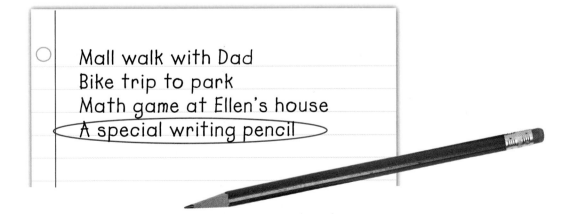

> ○
>
> Mall walk with Dad
> Bike trip to park
> Math game at Ellen's house
> (A special writing pencil)

4. **I fill in a story map. It helps me plan my writing.**

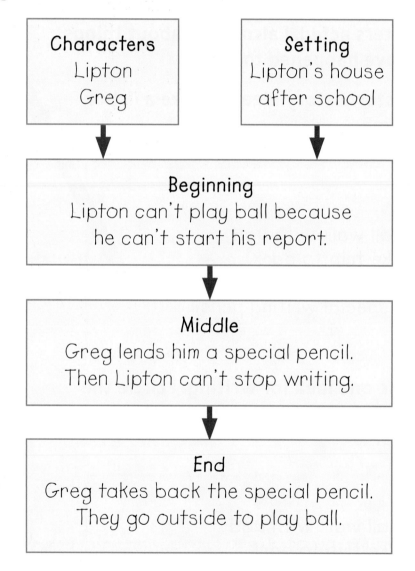

Characters	Setting
Lipton	Lipton's house
Greg	after school

Beginning
Lipton can't play ball because he can't start his report.

Middle
Greg lends him a special pencil. Then Lipton can't stop writing.

End
Greg takes back the special pencil. They go outside to play ball.

5. **I write my story. I revise it and give it a title.**

Here is a checklist I use when I write a story. You can use it when you write one, too.

Checklist for Writing a Story

☐ In the beginning I tell who the characters are and what the setting is.

☐ I make my story begin in an interesting way. One way to do this is to tell right away what the problem is.

☐ In the middle I tell what happens to the characters. I show what they do and how they feel.

☐ I use colorful adjectives to help make my writing clear.

☐ In the end I tell how the problem is solved.

☐ I make the end interesting by putting in a little surprise.

Contents

Setting... 54

Learn to identify when and where a story takes place.

Vocabulary...................................... 56

Read, write, and learn the meanings of new words.

Annie's Gifts by Angela Shelf Medearis
illustrated by Anna Rich 58

• Learn the features of realistic fiction.

• Read ahead to find out more about the story.

Sarah Enters a Painting by Susan Katz 88

Read a poem about a painting.

Connections 90

• Compare texts.

• Review phonics skills.

• Reread for fluency.

• Write about setting.

Lesson 17

Realistic Fiction

ANNIE'S GIFTS
by Angela Shelf Medearis

Illustrated by Anna Rich

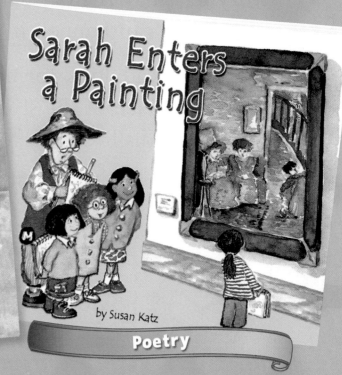

Sarah Enters
a Painting

by Susan Katz

Poetry

Focus Skill

 **Setting**

The **setting** is the time and place in which a story happens. A story can happen over any length of time. It can happen in one or more places.

As you read, look for details that tell the exact time and place of the story. This chart shows some setting details to watch for.

Setting	
When	Where
Season	City
Day of week	Street
Time of day	Kind of home

Think about why the setting is important in a story. Ask yourself how the story would be different if its setting were changed.

54

Read the story. Which words tell you when the story takes place?

Mr. Joseph's Jingle

Mr. Joseph jingles when he walks. That's because he always carries a lot of coins in his pockets. He doesn't go anywhere in the city without his pennies, nickels, dimes, and quarters.

Mr. Joseph needs quarters for the bus in the morning. He uses dimes to buy a newspaper at lunch. He gives the baker nickels for fresh bread for dinner. At the end of the day, he puts his pennies into a jar. When the jar is full, he gives it to the city's animal shelter.

Setting	
When	Where

Try This!

Look back at the story. What words tell where the story takes place?

GO online www.harcourtschool.com/reading

- except
- screeching
- stomped
- entertain
- carefree
- sipped

Cora's Violin

Cora's family played many instruments. In fact, they played every instrument that Cora knew **except** the violin. Cora wanted to be different, so she started violin lessons.

At first, Cora's violin made terrible **screeching** sounds when she tried to play. Some days she stopped practicing and **stomped** away. Slowly, she learned to play well.

Now Cora can play many beautiful songs. She likes to **entertain** her family by playing for them.

One day, Cora and her teacher, Mr. Miles, were playing some lively, **carefree** music. Suddenly, Cora's violin squawked. They soon saw the cause—a broken string.

Later, as Mr. Miles **sipped** his drink, Cora laughed. "You never know what surprises your violin has for you!" she said.

Word Champion

Your challenge this week is to use the Vocabulary Words while talking to others. For example, tell a classmate about something you do to **entertain** your family. Each day, write in your vocabulary journal the sentences you spoke.

GO online www.harcourtschool.com/reading

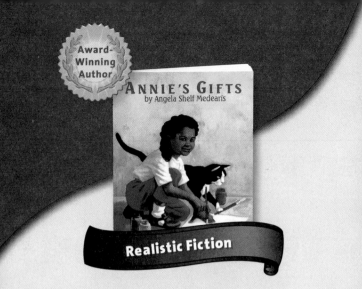
ANNIE'S GIFTS
by Angela Shelf Medearis

Realistic Fiction

Genre Study

Realistic fiction is a story that could really happen. Look for

- characters who do things real people do.
- a realistic setting.

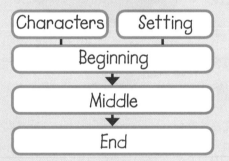

Characters	Setting
Beginning	
↓	
Middle	
↓	
End	

Comprehension Strategy

Monitor Comprehension— Read ahead to find out more if something does not make sense.

58

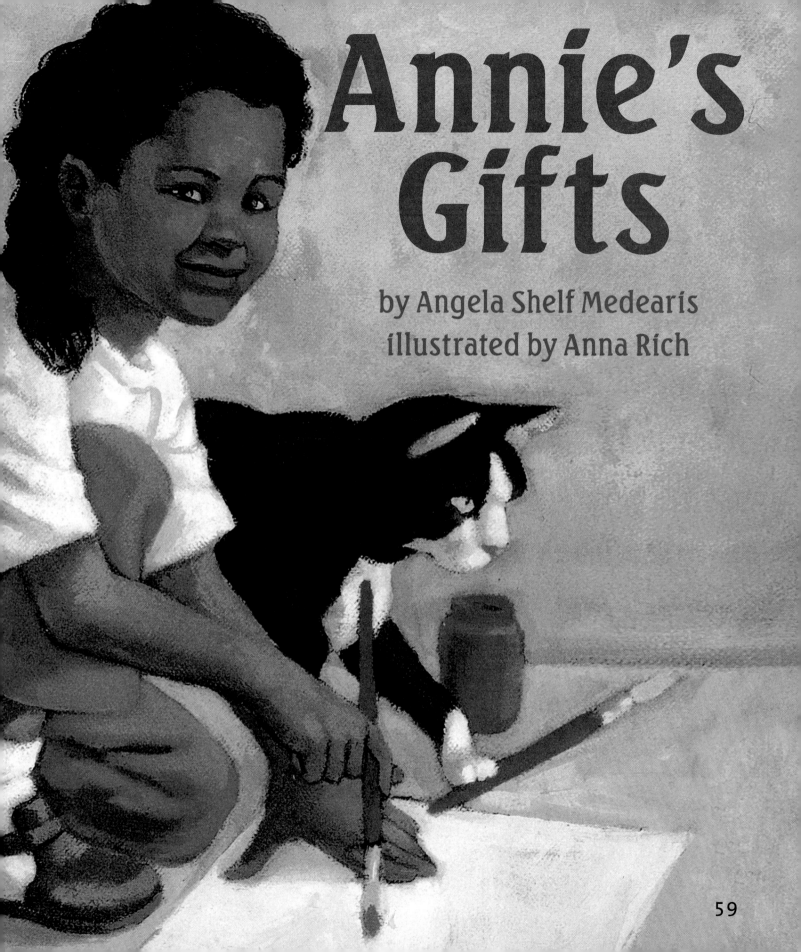

Annie's Gifts

by Angela Shelf Medearis

illustrated by Anna Rich

Once there lived a family that loved music. Every morning the children, Lee, Patty, and Annie, turned on some music. The floors trembled as they stomped their feet to the loud bass beat. Soon they were moving down the street to catch the school bus.

After the children left for school, Momma would turn on the radio. Momma swayed with the sweet rhythm as she sipped her coffee.

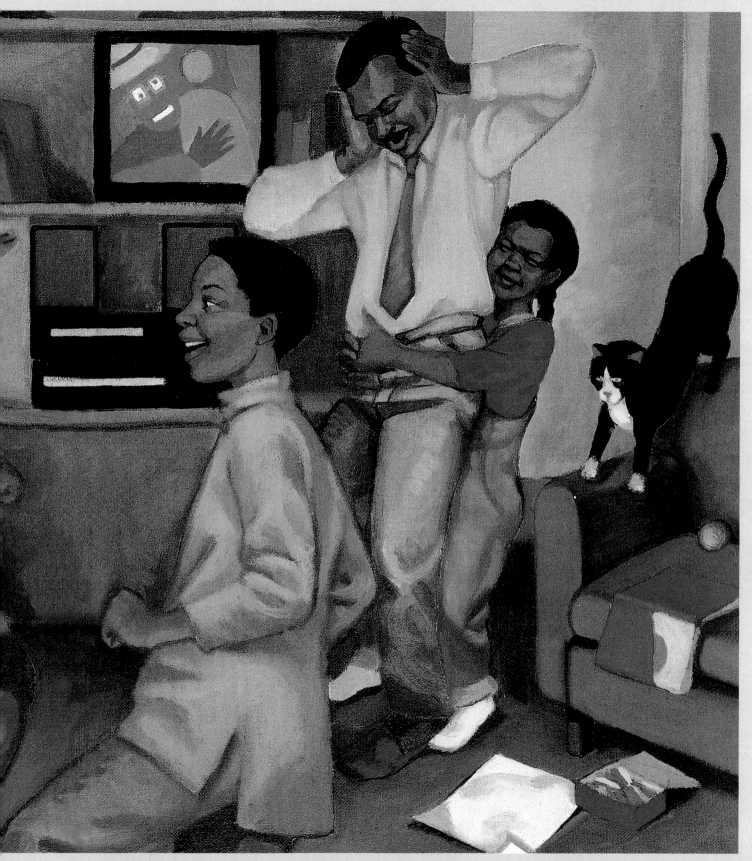

Every night, after the children were in bed, Daddy would say, "Come on, honey! Let's go once around the floor." Then he and Momma slow-danced to the soulful blues music he loved.

Lee loved music so much that he
joined his school band. Annie thought
Lee looked wonderful in his uniform
with the shiny brass buttons. Lee's
music sounded like the circus. When
he swung into a song on the trumpet,
Annie tapped her feet and clapped
her hands.

Patty was a wonderful musician, too. When Patty played the piano, it made Annie think of pretty colors, soft rain, and springtime flowers. Patty also had a lovely singing voice. When company came, she would entertain the guests.

"Wonderful, just wonderful," the guests would sigh and clap their hands after Patty's performance. Annie decided that she wanted to play an instrument, too.

One day, Annie's school music teacher, Mrs. Mason, passed out instruments to the class. She gave Annie a recorder.

The class practiced a group song for months. Everyone played their part perfectly, everyone except Annie. When Annie played, the recorder squeaked and squawked like chickens at feeding time.

"I don't think the recorder is the
instrument for you," Mrs. Mason said.
"I guess you're right," Annie said.
"Maybe I can play the cello."
"Let's give it a try," Mrs. Mason
said. "I'll show you how to play it."

When Mrs. Mason played the cello, it sounded warm and carefree, like carousel music. Annie tried and tried, but when she played the cello, it always sounded like a chorus of screeching alley cats.

"Oh," Mrs. Mason sighed and rubbed her ears. "Annie, darling, I just don't think this is the instrument for you. How would you like to make a banner and some posters announcing our program?"

"Okay," said Annie. She was disappointed, but she did love to draw. Annie drew while everyone else practiced.

That evening, Annie picked up Lee's trumpet and tried to play it. Her playing sounded like an elephant with a bad cold. Lee begged her to stop. Annie's feelings were hurt, but she put the trumpet away.

"I wish I could find an instrument to play," Annie told her mother.

"Cheer up!" Momma said. "We're going to get a new piano and everyone is going to take piano lessons!"

Soon, a beautiful, new piano was delivered to Annie's house. The piano was made of shiny, brown mahogany. Annie peeked under the piano lid while Patty played a song. "Melody Maker" was written in beautiful gold letters.

That week, all three children started piano lessons with Mrs. Kelly. After every lesson, Mrs. Kelly gave them new sheet music to practice.

Patty and Lee did very well. Mrs. Kelly always told them how talented they were.

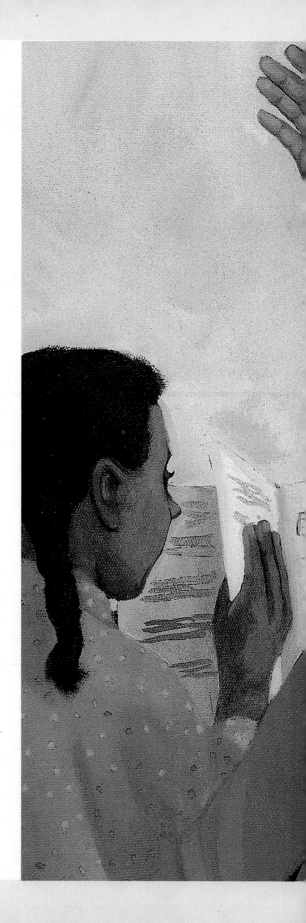

Oh, but when Annie played the piano, Mrs. Kelly's smile turned into a frown. The low notes sounded like a diesel truck honking its horn and the middle ones like croaking frogs. The high notes sobbed like a crying baby.

Once, Annie tried to sing and play the piano for her parents' guests. Her performance made everyone squirm in their chairs. Annie was so embarrassed that she went up to her room and cried. She couldn't play the recorder or the cello. She couldn't play the piano or sing or play the trumpet. Annie had never felt so sad in her life.

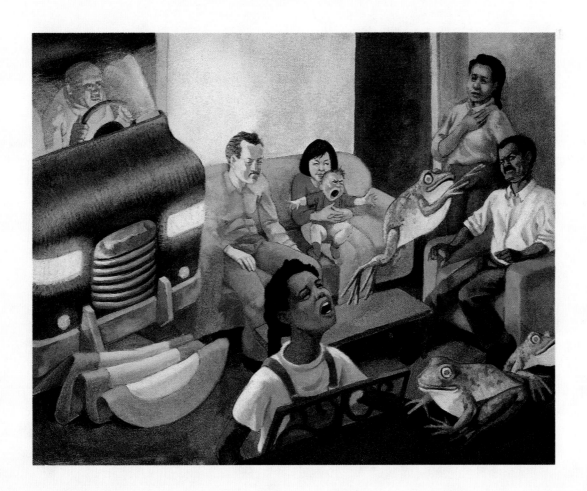

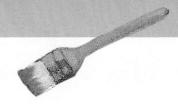

Sometimes when Annie was sad, she liked to write poetry to make herself feel better. She decided to write a poem about music.

I love to hear music play.
I practice hard every day.
But even though I try and try,
the sounds I play
make people laugh and cry.

That night, Annie put her poem on Daddy's pillow. Then she went to sleep.

In the morning, Daddy and Momma
had a long talk with Annie.

"I just can't seem to do anything right,"
Annie sighed.

"Yes, you can," Daddy said. "There are
lots of things you can do."

"Really, Daddy?" Annie asked.

"Of course," Momma said. "Not everyone
can play the piano and sing like Patty. Not
everyone can play the trumpet like Lee.
That's his special gift. And not everyone
can write poetry and draw beautiful
pictures the way you can."

"I didn't think about it that way," Annie said. "I can't sing or play an instrument well, but I can do *a lot* of other things."

Now, if you should pass by Annie's house, you might hear Patty singing and playing on the piano. Perhaps you'll hear Lee playing his trumpet. And sometimes, if you stop and listen very, very closely, you might hear Annie playing . . .

her radio!

Annie plays loud, finger-popping music when she feels like laughing and drawing pictures. She plays soft, sweet music when she writes her poems. She can play any kind of music she likes on her radio.

She still can't play the piano or sing like Patty, and she still can't play the trumpet like Lee.

But now Annie has found she's happiest when drawing her pictures and writing poetry. Because art and writing are Annie's gifts.

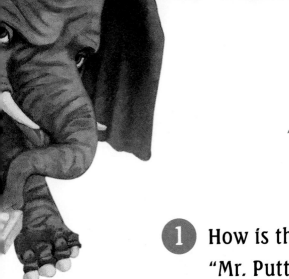

Think Critically

R3.1
W2.1b

1. How is the setting of this story like the setting of "Mr. Putter and Tabby Write the Book"? SETTING

2. How do you know that music is important to Annie's family? DRAW CONCLUSIONS

3. How does Annie feel when she finds her special talent? CHARACTERS' EMOTIONS

4. Why do you think the author says that Annie's music sounds like animals? AUTHOR'S CRAFT/IMAGERY

5. **WRITE** Annie does not give up easily. Use details from the story to show that Annie is a hard worker. EXTENDED RESPONSE

CALIFORNIA STANDARDS
ENGLISH-LANGUAGE ARTS STANDARDS—Reading 3.1 Compare and contrast plots, settings, and characters presented by different authors; **Writing 2.1b** Describe the setting, characters, objects, and events in detail.

Meet the Author
Angela Shelf Medearis

"Annie's Gifts" is based on Angela Shelf Medearis's life. Now that she has discovered her talent, she writes all the time.

Angela Shelf Medearis likes to make children laugh. What parts of the story do you think are funny?

Meet the Illustrator
Anna Rich

Anna Rich began to draw when she was young, and she has never stopped. She has illustrated many children's books, including two others by Angela Shelf Medearis.

Anna Rich likes to knit, sew, and, of course, paint. She says that when she reads a story, pictures appear in her brain.

www.harcourtschool.com/reading

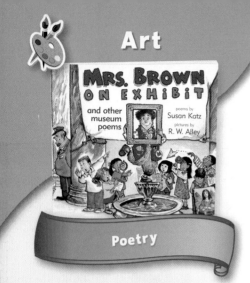

MRS. BROWN ON EXHIBIT
and other museum poems
poems by Susan Katz
pictures by R. W. Alley

Poetry

Sarah Enters a Painting

by Susan Katz
picture by R. W. Alley

If I stepped
into this painting,
I'd hurry past the grown-ups
dozing in their chairs
and rush up to the table
where that boy is reaching
for something I can't see from here.
A toy house? A train? A set of paints?
Maybe I'd stop
to play with him awhile.
And then I'd climb
that curved brown stair
to find out what
the painter hid way up there.

Connections

Comparing Texts

❶ How are "Annie's Gifts" and "Sarah Enters a Painting" alike? How are they different?

❷ What gift, or talent, would you most like to have? Why?

❸ What do you think your classmates enjoy the most—music, art, or writing? Explain.

Phonics R1.1

Guess the Word

With a group, think of short *e* words that have the letters *ea*. Write each word on a card. Then mix the cards, and place them face down. Take turns drawing a card and giving clues about the word. The person who guesses the word must spell it aloud.

bread

CALIFORNIA STANDARDS
ENGLISH-LANGUAGE ARTS STANDARDS—Reading 1.1 Recognize and use knowledge of spelling patterns (e.g., diphthongs, special vowel spellings) when reading; **Reading 1.6** Read aloud fluently and accurately and with appropriate intonation and expression; *(continued)*

Fluency Practice

R1.6

Read with a Partner

Work with a partner to perform a section of "Annie's Gifts" as Readers' Theater. Think about the most important words in each sentence. Read them in a clear, strong way.

Writing

W2.1b

Write About Setting

On a chart, list details about the setting of "Annie's Gifts." Then use your chart to help you write a description of the setting. Share your writing with a partner.

My Writing Checklist

Writing Trait → Organization

✔ My description is in an order that makes sense.

✔ I use a setting chart to plan my writing.

Setting	
When	Where

Reading 3.1 Compare and contrast plots, settings, and characters presented by different authors; Writing 2.1b Describe the setting, characters, objects, and events in detail.

Contents

Words with *oi* and *oy* 94

Learn to read words with *oi* and *oy*.

Vocabulary 96

Read, write, and learn the meanings of new words.

Ah, Music! by Aliki 98

• Learn the features of nonfiction.

• Answer questions by looking back at the selection.

Come, My Little Children, Here Are Songs for You by Robert Louis Stevenson
illustrated by Vladimir Radunsky 112

Read a classic poem about music.

Connections 114

• Compare texts.

• Review phonics skills.

• Reread for fluency.

• Write a paragraph.

Lesson 18

Nonfiction

Ah, Music!

Music to Sing & Play

Written and Illustrated by Aliki

Come, My Little Children, Here Are Songs for You

BY ROBERT LOUIS STEVENSON

Poetry

93

Phonics Skill

Words with *oi* and *oy*

The letters **oi** and **oy** stand for the sound at the end of *boy*. Read these words. Do they all have that sound?

noise   toy   soil   joy

Now read these longer words.

boiling   **enjoy**   **pointer**

Point to the letters in each word that stand for the vowel sound you hear in *boy*.

CALIFORNIA STANDARDS
ENGLISH-LANGUAGE ARTS STANDARDS—Reading 1.1 Recognize and use knowledge of spelling patterns (e.g., diphthongs, special vowel spellings) when reading.

Read each word on the left. Tell which word on the right has the same sound.

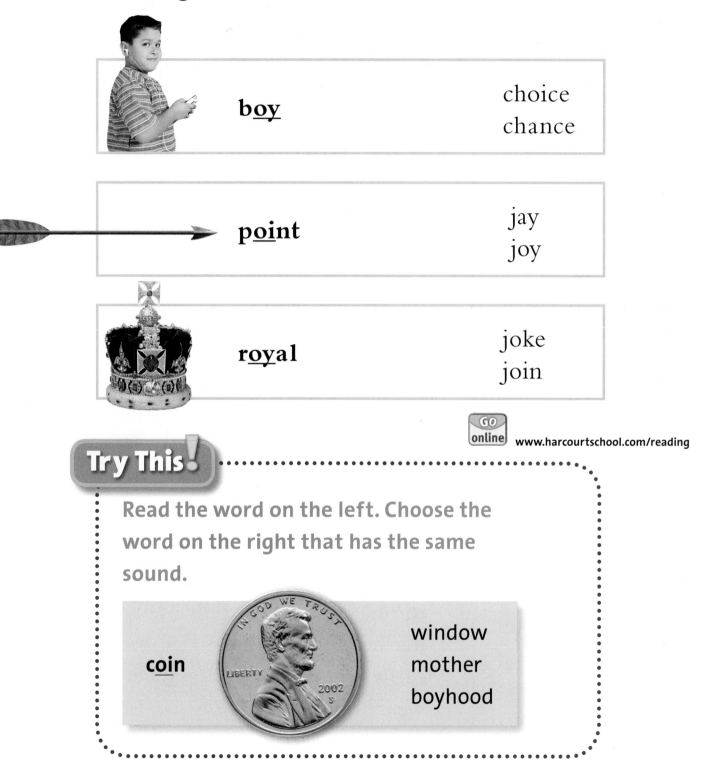

b<u>oy</u>

choice
chance

p<u>oi</u>nt

jay
joy

r<u>oy</u>al

joke
join

GO online www.harcourtschool.com/reading

Try This!

Read the word on the left. Choose the word on the right that has the same sound.

c<u>oi</u>n

window
mother
boyhood

95

relieved

volume

concentrate

performance

creative

expression

The Sounds of Music

Grandpa and I both love to listen to music, but we have a problem. We don't like the same kind of music. I'm always **relieved** when Grandpa turns his music off. I don't like opera music.

Grandpa feels the same way about my pop music. When I turn the **volume** up, he snorts and walks out of the room. Then Mom tells me to use my headphones. I don't mind. I can **concentrate** better when I'm wearing them.

One day, Mom surprised us. She had tickets for a **performance** of an opera. She also had tickets to a pop concert. She wanted Grandpa and me to see how **creative** both kinds of music can be.

I had to laugh when I saw the **expression** on Grandpa's face. I couldn't tell whether he was about to laugh or cry!

 www.harcourtschool.com/reading

Word Scribe

This week your task is to use the Vocabulary Words in your writing. For example, you might write a note that says "I'm **relieved** that we don't have a test today." At the end of each day, write in your vocabulary journal the sentences that had Vocabulary Words.

Nonfiction

Genre Study

Nonfiction gives facts about a topic. Look for

- main ideas and details.

- headings that tell what each section is about.

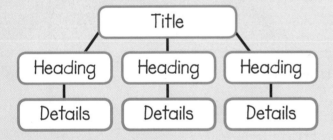

Title

Heading   Heading   Heading

Details   Details   Details

Comprehension Strategy

Answer questions by looking back at information in different parts of the selection.

CALIFORNIA STANDARDS
ENGLISH-LANGUAGE ARTS STANDARDS—
Reading 2.5 Restate facts and details in the text to clarify and organize ideas.

Ah, Music!

written and illustrated by
Aliki

Music Is Sound

If you hum a tune,

play an instrument,

or clap out a rhythm,

you are making music.
You are listening to it, too.

Music Is Rhythm

That is the beat I can clap.

Rhythm is a marching-band beat, a puffing-train beat,

a beating-the-eggs beat, a heart beat.
Some rhythm beats are stronger than others.
You can count the accents.

A person who cannot hear
can feel the vibration of the beat.

Music Is Melody

That is the tune I can hum,

or the song that is sung
if words are set to music.
Often the words are poetry.

Music Is Volume

That is the loudness or the softness of the sound.

Shhh.

Music Is Feeling

It sets a mood.

Music speaks not with words, as in a song.
It speaks with expression.
Everyone can understand music, because
everyone has feelings.
Music can make you feel happy or sad or scared.
It can make you want to dance, to march, to sing,
or to be quiet, to listen, and to dream.

Ah, music!

*Here will we sit
and let the sounds of music
creep in our ears.*

Shakespeare said that.

I listen to music,
and I can see pictures
in my head.

I imagine I hear
twittering birds.

I hear a cool waterfall.

I see a brilliant sunrise.

I see a scary dark forest.

I hear a noisy city.

Music Is a Creative Art

Just as a writer uses words,

or an artist uses paint,

a composer uses music
to create images and feelings.
He or she writes it down in notes, symbols,
and numbers on lines and spaces.
The notations describe the rhythm, tone, pitch,
feeling, and even the silences of the piece.

Practice Makes Perfect

We make music.
Making music is hard fun.
It takes lots of practice to learn
to play an instrument.

But when you do, it is forever.

That's the hard part.

Here's the fun part.

As you practice and learn,
you begin to make
beautiful sounds.
Practice becomes fun.

You learn new pieces to play.
You feel proud.
Your music teacher says
you will play in a recital.
You will play for an audience.

A metronome
helps keep time.

The Performance

she must be nervous.

At your recital it is your turn to play.
Everyone is looking at you.

You **concentrate**.
You do the best you can.

When you finish, everyone claps.
It sounds like waves breaking.
It feels good. You take a bow.
You feel **relieved** and very proud.

You celebrate.
Everyone says you did well.
Next time it will be even
better, because you are
learning more every day.
Practice makes perfect.

Music Is for Everybody

Think Critically

R2.1
R2.3
R2.5
W1.1

1 Under what heading would you look to find examples of rhythm? **LOCATE INFORMATION**

2 What are some ways music can make you feel? IMPORTANT DETAILS

3 What do you think the author means when she says that making music is "hard fun"?

DRAW CONCLUSIONS

4 Why might it be important to play in a recital? DRAW CONCLUSIONS

5 **WRITE** How are a composer, a writer, and an artist alike? Use details from the selection to support your answer.

SHORT RESPONSE

CALIFORNIA STANDARDS
ENGLISH-LANGUAGE ARTS STANDARDS—Reading 2.1 Use titles, tables of contents, and chapter headings to locate information in expository text; **Reading 2.3** Use knowledge of the author's purpose(s) to comprehend informational text; **Reading 2.5** Restate facts and details in the text to clarify and organize ideas; **Writing 1.1** Group related ideas and maintain a consistent focus.

Aliki

Ever since she was a young girl, Aliki has been writing down her feelings. She thinks that doing this was good practice for when she became an author.

"Ah, Music!" took over three years for Aliki to write and draw. She had to do a lot of studying to find out about music and what different instruments looked like.

GO online www.harcourtschool.com/reading

111

Poetry

Come, My Little Children, Here Are Songs for You

BY ROBERT LOUIS STEVENSON
ILLUSTRATED BY VLADIMIR RADUNSKY

Come, my little children, here are songs for you;
Some are short and some are long and all, all are new.
You must learn to sing them very small and clear,
Very true to time and tune and pleasing to the ear.

112

Mark the note that rises, mark the notes that fall.
Mark the time when broken, and the swing of it all.
So when night is come and you have gone to bed,
All the songs you love to sing shall echo in your head.

Connections

Comparing Texts

1 How are "Ah, Music!" and "Come, My Little Children, Here Are Songs for You" alike? How are they different?

2 What instrument and what song would you like to play at a recital? Why?

3 What other activities are both hard and fun?

Phonics

Reading Words

Think of eight words that have the letters *oi* and *oy*. Write each word on a card. Trade cards with a partner. Who can read the words the fastest without mistakes?

Fluency Practice

R1.6

Read Naturally

Choose a section of "Ah, Music!" to read aloud. Read the phrases in the section the way you would say them if you were talking to a friend. Practice reading the section several times.

Writing

W1.1

Write a Paragraph

Think of a children's song. Write a paragraph explaining what you see, hear, imagine, and feel when you hear this song. Share your paragraph with a classmate

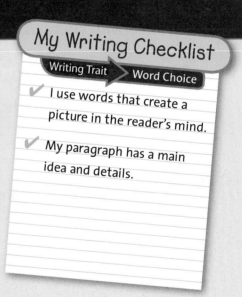

My Writing Checklist

Writing Trait ➤ Word Choice

✔ I use words that create a picture in the reader's mind.

✔ My paragraph has a main idea and details.

When I hear "Twinkle, Twinkle Little Star," I see stars sprinkled across the sky.

Contents

Locate Information 118

Learn how to use a table of contents and chapter titles to locate information.

Vocabulary 120

Read, write, and learn the meanings of new words.

**The Life of
George Washington Carver** by Joli K. Stevens 122

• Learn the features of a biography.

• Answer questions by looking back at the selection.

Nutty Facts About Peanuts from *Ranger Rick* 136

Read a magazine article about peanuts.

Connections 138

• Compare texts.

• Review phonics skills.

• Reread for fluency.

• Write a description.

Lesson 19

Biography

The Life of George Washington Carver

by Joli K. Stevens

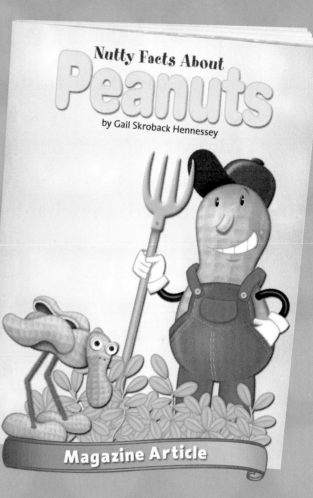

Nutty Facts About **Peanuts**

by Gail Skroback Hennessey

Magazine Article

Focus Skill

 ## Locate Information

You can use a **table of contents** at the beginning of a book to help you find information. Many tables of contents list **chapters** in a book and the page number on which each chapter begins. The title of the chapter gives you a clue about what you will read in that chapter.

The Life of Dr. Martin Luther King, Jr.
Table of Contents
Chapter 1: The Early Years . . . . .page 1
Chapter 2: Minister and Leader . . . . .page 8
Chapter 3: Nobel Prize Winner . . . . . . .page 15

CALIFORNIA STANDARDS
ENGLISH-LANGUAGE ARTS STANDARDS—Reading 2.1 Use titles, tables of contents, and chapter headings to locate information in expository text.

Read the table of contents below. Tell about the information that might be found in the second chapter.

The Life of Abraham Lincoln Table of Contents		

Chapter 1: Log Cabin Boy . . . . page 1
Chapter 2: Midwest Lawyer . . . . page 5
Chapter 3: President Lincoln . . . . . . page 9

Chapter Title	Information
Log Cabin Boy	Tells about Abraham Lincoln's childhood
Midwest Lawyer	
President Lincoln	

Try This!

Look back at the table of contents. What information will you find in Chapter 3?

 www.harcourtschool.com/reading

119

Vocabulary

crop

provide

supplies

experiments

committee

earn

Peanuts

Peanut plants are an important **crop** in the United States. Florida, Georgia, and Alabama **provide** most of the country's peanuts.

You may have the **supplies** at home to make peanut butter and jelly sandwiches. Many people think that is the best way to eat peanuts. There are many other ways, too.

Every year, scientists do **experiments** with peanuts. They find new kinds of peanuts for farmers to grow and sell. A **committee** of food experts then decides which peanuts taste the best.

Peanuts can be roasted, boiled, used raw, or ground up into peanut butter. Peanut farmers can **earn** money by growing peanuts because people want to buy them.

GO online www.harcourtschool.com/reading

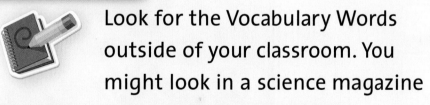

Word Detective

Look for the Vocabulary Words outside of your classroom. You might look in a science magazine or watch a science show on television. In your vocabulary journal, write the words you see or hear. Happy word hunting!

121

Biography

Genre Study

A **biography** is the story of a person's life. Look for

- events in time order.

- headings that tell what each section is about.

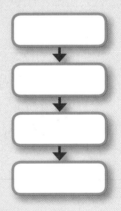

Comprehension Strategy

Answer questions by looking back at the information you read in the selection.

THE LIFE OF
George Washington Carver

BY JOLI K. STEVENS

George Washington Carver

A long time ago, people didn't eat peanuts. Peanuts were used only to feed animals. A man named George Washington Carver changed that. This is his story.

Childhood

George Washington Carver was born around 1864 in Missouri. George and his brother, James, were raised by Moses and Susan Carver. The Carvers did not have children of their own. The boys called the Carvers Uncle Moses and Aunt Susan.

George Washington Carver as a young boy

The Moses Carver House near Diamond
Grove, Newton County, Missouri

George was often sick as a child. Instead of
doing farm work, he helped in the house.

George had his own garden. He liked to care
for sick plants and make them healthy. People
began to call George "the plant doctor."

George liked to learn about the world around him. Aunt Susan taught him to read and write, but he wanted to know more. He was always asking questions. He wanted to go to school, but the closest school for African American children was many miles away.

School Days

When George was about 12, he set off for Lincoln School, 8 miles away. He learned all that school could teach him. Then he knew he must find a new school to be able to keep learning.

George was about 16 when he moved to Fort Scott, Kansas. From then on, he moved from place to place to earn money for school by doing odd jobs. He had to pay for his books and school supplies himself. In one town, he found that another person named George Carver was living there. So he added a *W* to his own name. "It is for Washington," he told his friends. George Washington Carver became his new name.

Lincoln School was a
one-room schoolhouse
like this one.

Not many African Americans went to college in the 1890s. George Washington Carver had to save money for college until he was almost 30 years old. He finally entered Simpson College, in Iowa, where he studied art. Later he went to Iowa State College to study science. He was asked to become a teacher there.

Teacher and Scientist

The president of Tuskegee Institute, Booker T. Washington, soon heard about George Washington Carver. He asked him to teach at Tuskegee, in Alabama. Tuskegee had poor land and poor farmers all around it. George Washington Carver saw that he could help. He got to work right away.

George Washington Carver's graduation photo from Iowa State College in 1894

George Washington Carver belonged to this group, the Welch Eclectic Society, while he was a student at Iowa State College

The teacher and his students
in a science class at the
Tuskegee Institute

George Washington Carver's students are examining mustard plants.

A mounted peanut plant collected by George Washington Carver

George Washington Carver taught his students that changing crops in a field help the plants grow better.

He started with the soil. He saw that too many
farmers were planting cotton. Planting the same
crop every year had made the soil poor.

George Washington Carver studied other crops
to see what would grow well and provide food
and money for the farmers. He told the farmers
to plant peanuts, cowpeas, and sweet potatoes.
Those crops would put good things back into the
soil. He said that the soil would be better if many
things were planted. The farmers didn't want to
plant new things. They were afraid that no one
would buy them.

George Washington Carver discovered that the boll weevil, an insect that eats cotton, would not eat peanuts or sweet potatoes. He found nearly 300 ways to use peanuts. They could be used to make peanut butter, flour, cheese, candy, shampoo, glue, ink, soap, and coffee. He also found more than 100 ways to use sweet potatoes. Soon the farmers started planting these crops.

George Washington Carver at work

George Washington Carver's typewriter

Plant materials had to be studied closely.

People wanted to pay George Washington Carver a lot of money to come and work for them. He always said no. Money was not important to him. He decided to use his savings to help people continue his work even after he died. He also started a museum that held many of the things he had made in his lab. He won many awards for his work. He was even asked to speak to a committee of the United States Congress about peanuts and sweet potatoes.

133

George Washington Carver died on January 5, 1943, when he was almost 80 years old. He was buried at Tuskegee Institute.

In 1946, the United States Congress named January 5 George Washington Carver Day. He once said, "Know science and science shall set you free, because science is truth." The truth is that George Washington Carver helped make the world a better place through his experiments and teaching.

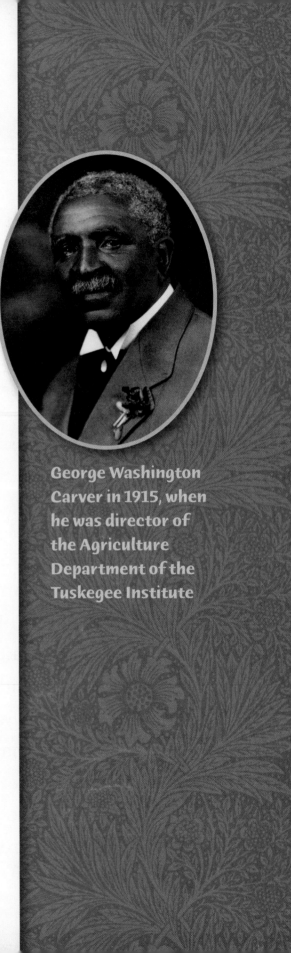

George Washington Carver in 1915, when he was director of the Agriculture Department of the Tuskegee Institute

This bronze sculpture honors the famous scientist and teacher

134

Think Critically

R2.1
R2.5
W1.1

1 Under which heading can you find information about the schools George Washington Carver attended?

 LOCATE INFORMATION

2 Why did some people call George Washington Carver "the plant doctor"?

IMPORTANT DETAILS

3 What tells you that he was a good student?

MAKE INFERENCES

4 Why was it important to farmers that George Washington Carver found many ways to use peanuts? DRAW CONCLUSIONS

5 **WRITE** Why does an inventor like George Washington Carver need to be creative? Use details from the selection to support your answer. SHORT RESPONSE

CALIFORNIA STANDARDS
ENGLISH-LANGUAGE ARTS STANDARDS—Reading 2.1 Use titles, tables of contents, and chapter headings to locate information in expository text; **Reading 2.5** Restate facts and details in the text to clarify and organize ideas; **Writing 1.1** Group related ideas and maintain a consistent focus.

Nutty Facts About
Peanuts

by Gail Skroback Hennessey

Not a Nut, But a Pea

The next time you are taking a big lick of peanut butter, you can say that you are eating your vegetables. Peanuts are not really nuts but are close cousins of peas and beans.

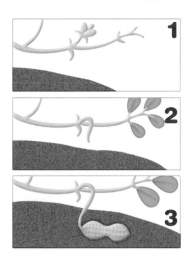

Down-Under Wonder

Peanuts grow down, not up! First, a flower on a peanut plant is pollinated. Next, a tiny stem grows down toward the soil. Once it has pushed into the ground, its tip swells and grows into a pod. Usually two seeds form inside the pod. Then the pods can be dug up.

Digital Peanuts

2
The number of presidents who were peanut farmers.

6
The number of pounds of peanuts eaten by each person in the United States each year.

9
The number of states that have big peanut crops. Georgia grows the most.

300
The number of products that George Washington Carver made from the peanut plant. Some of these are shampoo, ink, plastic, and ice cream.

720
The number of peanuts needed to make a one-pound jar of peanut butter.

1,500
The number of peanut butter sandwiches the average American child has eaten by the time he or she finishes high school.

7 million
The pounds of peanut butter eaten each year by people in the United States.

Connections

Comparing Texts

1 How can "Nutty Facts About Peanuts" help you understand "The Life of George Washington Carver"?

2 What kinds of experiments have you done?

3 What kinds of problems do today's scientists want to solve?

Phonics
R1.1

Write a Poem

Think of words that have the letters *ear* and *eer*. Use these words to make a rhyming poem. Then read your poem to a classmate.

I'd like to see a <u>deer</u>

come to me without <u>fear.</u>

I know I'd want to <u>cheer</u>

if a deer did come <u>near.</u>

CALIFORNIA STANDARDS
ENGLISH-LANGUAGE ARTS STANDARDS—Reading 1.1 Recognize and use knowledge of spelling patterns (e.g., diphthongs, special vowel spellings) when reading; **Reading 1.6** Read aloud fluently and accurately and with appropriate intonation and expression; **Writing 1.1** Group related ideas and maintain a consistent focus.

Fluency Practice

R1.6

Read Accurately

Choose a section of "The Life of George Washington Carver." Practice reading it aloud as a classmate follows along. Ask your classmate to point out words that you need to practice reading correctly.

Writing

W1.1

Write a Personal Narrative

Think about events in your life that are important to you. Write about them in the order in which they happened.

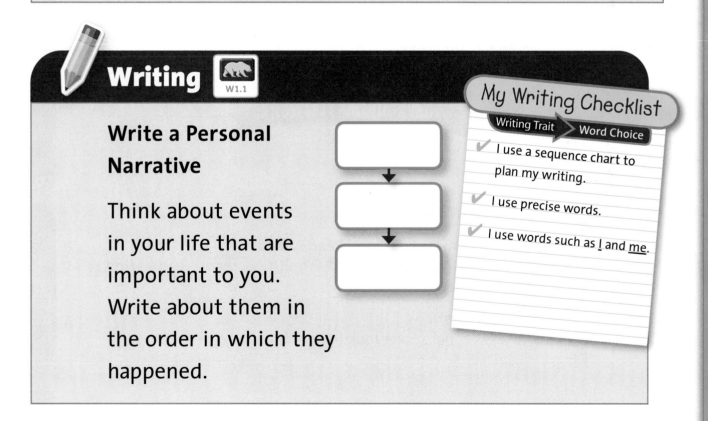

My Writing Checklist

Writing Trait → Word Choice

✔ I use a sequence chart to plan my writing.

✔ I use precise words.

✔ I use words such as <u>I</u> and <u>me</u>.

Contents

Game Show

READERS' THEATER

What's My Job?...142

Build Fluency
• Let your voice rise and fall to sound like natural speech.
• Read words accurately and correct yourself if you make a mistake.

Build Vocabulary
• Read, write, and learn the meanings of new words.

Review Vocabulary
• Read theme vocabulary words in a different context.

COMPREHENSION STRATEGIES
Review

Social Studies Textbook

North America...154

 ### Monitor Comprehension—Read Ahead
• When you don't understand something, read ahead to find out more.

 ### Answer Questions
• To answer questions, look back in the story.

Lesson 20

Theme Review and Vocabulary Builder

Readers' Theater
GAME SHOW

WHAT'S MY JOB?

Mystery Guest ?

Content-Area Reading
SOCIAL STUDIES TEXTBOOK

YOUR
Social Studies
TEXTBOOK

141

sleuths

host

responds

accurately

risk

statue

Reading for Fluency

When you read a script aloud,

- make your voice go up and down to help you read with expression.

- take time to read each word correctly.

WHAT'S

Characters

Announcer	Player 2
Host	Player 3
Player 1	Mystery Guest

MY JOB?

Setting

The set of a television game show

Announcer: Good morning, everyone! Welcome to "What's My Job?"—the game show in which super sleuths use their super detective skills. Here's the host of our show, Sandy Beach, to entertain us.

Host: Good morning! Let's get started. I think most of you have already watched "What's My Job?" For those who haven't, here are the rules.

143

Announcer: "What's My Job?" is easy to play. Each player takes a turn asking our Mystery Guest a question about his or her job. After our guest responds, the players can try to guess the job of our Mystery Guest. The players have only three guesses. They need to use them wisely.

Host: Here's the exciting part. Whoever guesses accurately wins a special prize!

Player 1: A special prize!

Player 2: I know I'm going to win it!

Player 3: I wouldn't be so sure about that.

Host: Now, let's meet our special guest. Mystery Guest, welcome to the show.

Mystery Guest: Thank you. I'm happy to be here.

Host: Are you ready to get started?

Mystery Guest: Yes, I am. Do you know what my job is?

Host: That's not for me to figure out. That's why we have our players. Now, let's begin. The first question, please.

Player 1: Mystery Guest, do you make things?

Fluency Tip

Read each word carefully.

Mystery Guest

145

Mystery Guest: Yes, I do.

Player 2: Oh, I know what your job is!

Host: Don't you think you should ask a question first, Player 2?

Player 2: Okay. Mystery Guest, do you make something that people ride in?

Mystery Guest: No, I don't.

Player 2: Really? Well, I guess I don't know what your job is, after all.

Host: Player 3, what is your question for our Mystery Guest?

Player 3: Mystery Guest, do you make something that people enjoy by using their senses?

Mystery Guest: Yes, I do.

Host: Aha! That means seeing, feeling, smelling, hearing, and tasting. It sounds as if you do something creative. Are there any guesses from our players?

Player 2: I know! You make music. You are a musician!

Mystery Guest: No, I'm not.

Fluency Tip

Player 2 is always in a hurry to answer. How should you read these lines?

147

Host: Good try, Player 2. Better luck next time. Back to you, Player 1. What is your second question for our Mystery Guest?

Player 1: Mystery Guest, do you use tools to make things?

Mystery Guest: Yes, I do.

Player 2: Ooh! Ooh! I think I know! Do you use a hammer?

Mystery Guest: Yes, I do.

Player 2: I have another guess!

Host: Remember, there are only two guesses left. Are you ready to risk a second one?

Player 2: Of course I am. It's not much of a risk when you know you're right. Mystery Guest, you are a carpenter!

Mystery Guest: No, I'm not.

Player 2: Ahhhh! Wrong again!

Host: That's another guess gone for our players. Now there's only one left. Player 3, it's your turn to ask a question.

Player 3: Mystery Guest, do you make things out of wood?

Mystery Guest: No, I don't.

Host: Let's review what we know so far. You make things that people use some of their senses to enjoy. You use a hammer, but you don't make things out of wood. This is hard to figure out.

Announcer: I know I can't figure it out. We're lucky we have a committee of expert detectives to work on it!

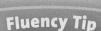

Fluency Tip

Reading slowly and carefully will help you read accurately.

149

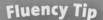

Fluency Tip

How do you think Players 1 and 2 should sound if they are annoyed?

Player 2: I know what it is! I know what it is! You are a . . .

Player 3: Wait! Player 2, don't use up our last guess!

Player 1: Please give someone else a chance, Player 2.

Player 2: Okay.

Player 1: I have one more question. Mystery Guest, do you make things out of stone?

Mystery Guest: Yes, I do.

Player 2: I know! It's easy!

Player 1: Wait, Player 2! I think I know what the Mystery Guest does, but I don't want to take a chance with the last guess.

Host: I think the players would like to have one of those guesses back now.

Player 2: All I need is one last question. Mystery Guest, do you make art?

Mystery Guest: Yes, I do.

Fluency Tip

Breaking the announcer's long part into shorter sections will make it easier to read.

Player 3: You're a sculptor!

Mystery Guest: Yes, I am a sculptor!

Player 2: That's what I was going to say!

Host: I'm sorry, Player 2, we can have only one winner.

Announcer: That was good detective work, Player 3. You concentrated on the clues. A sculptor uses a hammer to make a statue out of stone, and statues are art! A sculptor can sell art to people who want it for their homes or businesses.

Host: Actually, all of our players did a great job, but Player 3 earned the prize.

CLAP CLAP CLAP

WINNER

152

Announcer: Let's put our hands together and clap for our Mystery Guest, too. We want to thank you for being on our show.

Mystery Guest: I really liked the show. It was a lot of fun!

Host: By the way, Player 3, do you like art?

Player 3: I sure do.

Host: That's good, because your prize is a statue made by our Mystery Guest! Here it is! Aren't you thrilled?

Player 2: I'm startled. The statue looks just like you.

Host: That's because it is me—Sandy Beach, your carefree game show host. Now that's art!

COMPREHENSION STRATEGIES
Review

Reading Your Social Studies Book

Bridge to Content-Area Reading Social studies books have special features that help you read for information. Some of these are titles, special vocabulary, and maps.

Read the notes on page 155. How can the features help you read?

Review the Focus Strategies R2.5

You can also use the strategies you learned in this theme to help you read.

Monitor Comprehension—Read Ahead
If something you are reading does not make sense, read ahead to gather more information.

Answer Questions
Use information from what you read to answer questions. Look back in the text to check your answers.

Use comprehension strategies as you read "North America" on pages 156–157.

CALIFORNIA STANDARDS
ENGLISH-LANGUAGE ARTS STANDARDS—Reading 2.5 Restate facts and details in the text to clarify and organize ideas.

TITLE
The title tells what the lesson will be about.

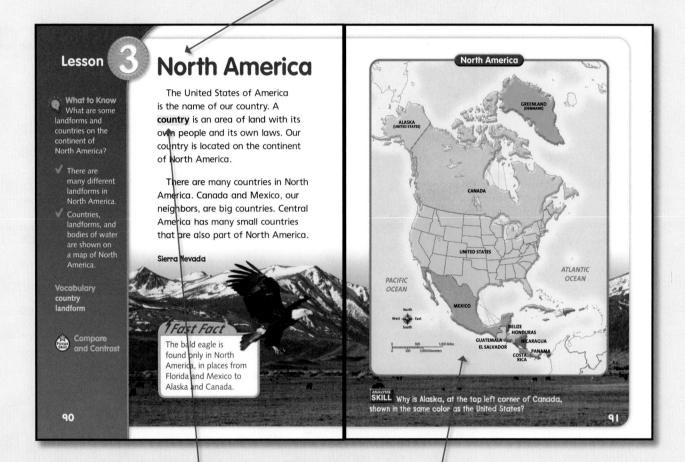

Lesson 3 **North America**

What to Know
What are some landforms and countries on the continent of North America?

✓ There are many different landforms in North America.

✓ Countries, landforms, and bodies of water are shown on a map of North America.

Vocabulary
country
landform

Compare and Contrast

The United States of America is the name of our country. A **country** is an area of land with its own people and its own laws. Our country is located on the continent of North America.

There are many countries in North America. Canada and Mexico, our neighbors, are big countries. Central America has many small countries that are also part of North America.

Sierra Nevada

Fast Fact
The bald eagle is found only in North America, in places from Florida and Mexico to Alaska and Canada.

90

North America

GREENLAND (DENMARK)
ALASKA (UNITED STATES)
CANADA
UNITED STATES
PACIFIC OCEAN
ATLANTIC OCEAN
MEXICO
BELIZE
HONDURAS
GUATEMALA
EL SALVADOR
NICARAGUA
COSTA RICA
PANAMA

North / West / East / South

0   500   1,000 Miles
0   500   1,000 Kilometers

ANALYSIS SKILL Why is Alaska, at the top left corner of Canada, shown in the same color as the United States?

91

VOCABULARY
New vocabulary words are in dark print. The meaning of the word is explained in the sentence. Vocabulary words are also in the glossary in the back of your social studies book.

MAP
Maps give you information about the places in the lesson. Use the compass rose to find north, south, east, and west.

155

Apply the Strategies Read these pages from a social studies book. As you read, stop and think about how you are using comprehension strategies.

Lesson 3

North America

What to Know
What are some landforms and countries on the continent of North America?

✔ There are many different landforms in North America.

✔ Countries, landforms, and bodies of water are shown on a map of North America.

Vocabulary
country
landform

Focus Skill Compare and Contrast

The United States of America is the name of our country. A **country** is an area of land with its own people and its own laws. Our country is located on the continent of North America.

There are many countries in North America. Canada and Mexico, our neighbors, are big countries. Central America has many small countries that are also part of North America.

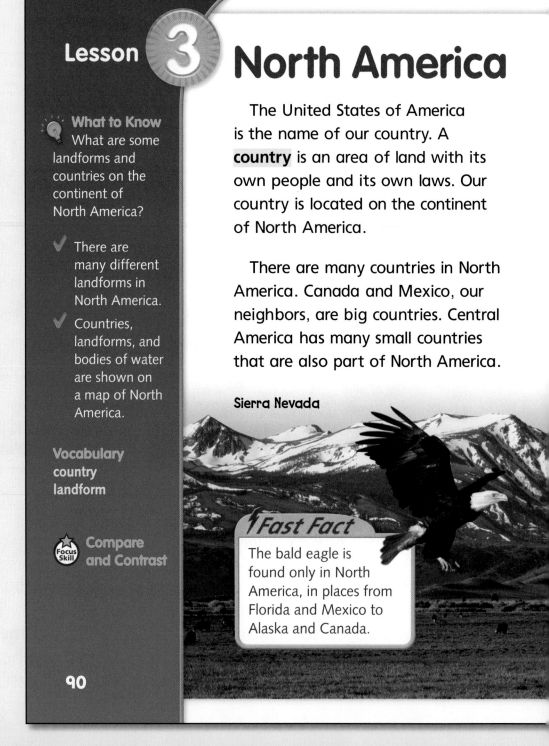

Sierra Nevada

Fast Fact
The bald eagle is found only in North America, in places from Florida and Mexico to Alaska and Canada.

Stop and Think

How could reading ahead help you answer the question at the bottom of the page?

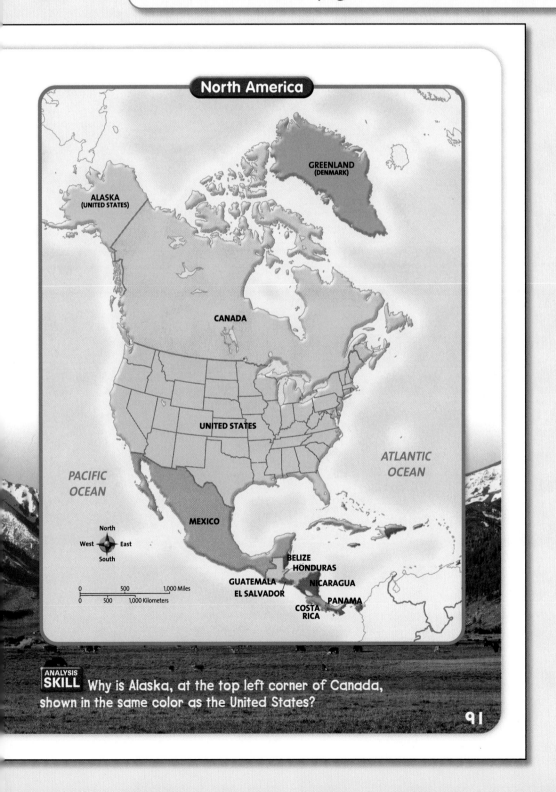

North America

GREENLAND
(DENMARK)

ALASKA
(UNITED STATES)

CANADA

UNITED STATES

ATLANTIC
OCEAN

PACIFIC
OCEAN

North

West ✦ East

South

MEXICO

BELIZE
HONDURAS

0   500   1,000 Miles

0   500   1,000 Kilometers

GUATEMALA   NICARAGUA
EL SALVADOR

COSTA
RICA

PANAMA

ANALYSIS SKILL Why is Alaska, at the top left corner of Canada, shown in the same color as the United States?

91

READING-WRITING
CONNECTION

Lesson 21 >

Lesson 22 >

Selection Titles	**A Chair For My Mother** Saving Money	**Serious Farm** Beyond Old MacDonald
Comprehension Strategies	Use Story Structure	Use Story Structure
Focus Skills	Plot	Plot

158

Theme (5) Better Together

Balloons for a Dime, Jonathan Green

Lesson 23 ▶

The Bee
California Bee Business

Summarize

Words with *oo, ew, ue, ui, ou*

Reading 1.1 Recognize and use
knowledge of spelling patterns
(e.g., diphthongs, special vowel spellings) when
reading; **Reading 2.5** Restate facts and details
in the text to clarify and organize ideas.

Lesson 24 ▶

Watching in the Wild
Chimp Computer Whiz

Summarize

Use Graphic Aids

Reading 2.5 Restate facts and details
in the text to clarify and organize
ideas; **Reading 2.7** Interpret information from
diagrams, charts, and graphs.

Lesson 25 (Review)

Town Hall
A Time For Patience

Review Skills and Strategies

Reading 1.1 Recognize and use
knowledge of spelling patterns
(e.g., diphthongs, special vowel spellings) when
reading; **Reading 2.5** Restate facts and details
in the text to clarify and organize ideas; **Reading
2.7** Interpret information from diagrams,
charts, and graphs.

Contents

Plot 162

Learn about the problem and solution in a story.

Vocabulary. 164

Read, write, and learn the meanings of new words.

A Chair for My Mother by Vera B. Williams 166

• Learn the features of realistic fiction.

• Use story structure to understand what you are reading.

Saving Money by Mary Firestone 192

Read about a girl who is learning to save money.

Connections 196

• Compare texts.

• Review phonics skills.

• Reread for fluency.

• Write a story.

Lesson 21

Realistic Fiction

Vera B. Williams

A CHAIR FOR MY MOTHER

Saving Money
by Mary Firestone

Nonfiction

Focus Skill

 Plot R2.5

Every story has characters, a setting, and a plot. The **plot** is what happens during the beginning, middle, and end of a story.

- The beginning introduces the characters and tells about a problem they have.

- The middle tells how they deal with the problem.

- The end tells how they solve it.

Read this story map. What problem does Ashley have? How does she solve it?

> **Problem**
> Ashley wants a new bicycle. She doesn't have enough money to buy one.

⬇

> **Important Events**
> Ashley helps her brother do yard work. He pays her. She saves her money.

⬇

> **Solution**
> Ashley saves enough money to buy a bicycle.

Read this story. What problem does the character have?

A Present for Mom

Mom's birthday was coming. Jill wanted to buy her flowers, but she had saved only $1.89. That wasn't enough for the flowers.

Then Jill had an idea. She would make some lemonade and set up a lemonade stand. After one day, Jill had made ten dollars. Now she could buy her mom flowers for her birthday.

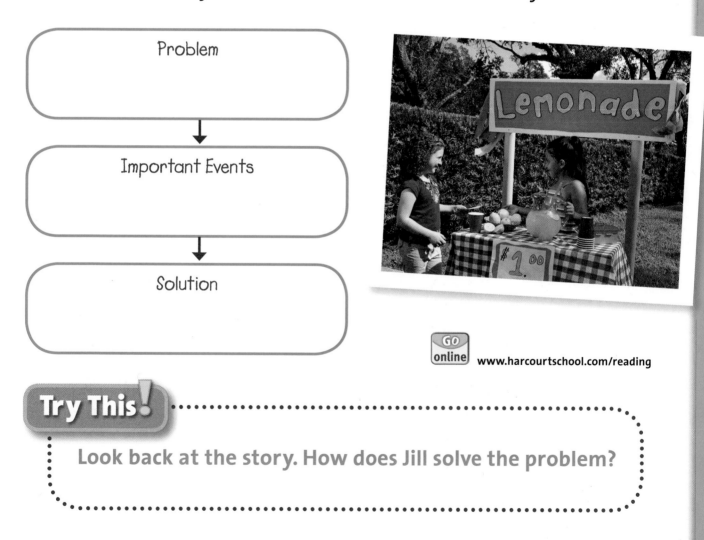

Problem

Important Events

Solution

GO online www.harcourtschool.com/reading

Try This!

Look back at the story. How does Jill solve the problem?

Vocabulary

bargain

delivered

spoiled

boost

comfortable

exchanged

A Special Sale

The sign in the shop window said, "Sale! All shoes half price!"

"What a great **bargain**!" Mom said to Taylor. "You need new shoes."

Inside the shop, the shelves were stacked. The salesclerk said, "These shoes were just **delivered** for our sale!"

Taylor found a pair of shoes she liked. Then she looked at them closely. "Oh no! These shoes are **spoiled** by a stain!"

SALE PRICE

164

Then Taylor saw a second pair just like them, high up on a shelf. Mom had to **boost** Taylor up to see them.

The shoes looked perfect! Taylor tried them on. "These shoes are **comfortable**!" she said.

Mom took the shoes to the salesclerk. She **exchanged** her money for the store's shoes. Taylor wore her new shoes home!

 www.harcourtschool.com/reading

Word Detective

Be a word detective! Look and listen to find the Vocabulary Words in the world around you. Write the words in your vocabulary journal. Tell where you found them.

Vera B. Williams

A CHAIR FOR MY MOTHER

Realistic Fiction

Genre Study

Realistic fiction is a story that could really happen. Look for

- a plot that could be real.
- a problem that needs to be solved.

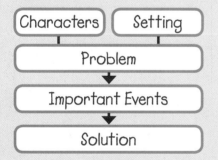

Characters — Setting

Problem

Important Events

Solution

R2.5

Comprehension Strategy

Use story structure to help you think about the important events in the plot.

CALIFORNIA STANDARDS
ENGLISH-LANGUAGE ARTS STANDARDS—
Reading 2.5 Restate facts and details in the text to clarify and organize ideas.

166

A CHAIR

FOR MY MOTHER

by
Vera B. Williams

My mother works as a waitress in the Blue Tile Diner. After school sometimes I go to meet her there. Then her boss, Josephine, gives me a job too.

I wash the salts and peppers and fill the ketchups. One time I peeled all the onions for the onion soup. When I finish, Josephine says, "Good work, honey," and pays me. And every time, I put half of my money into the jar.

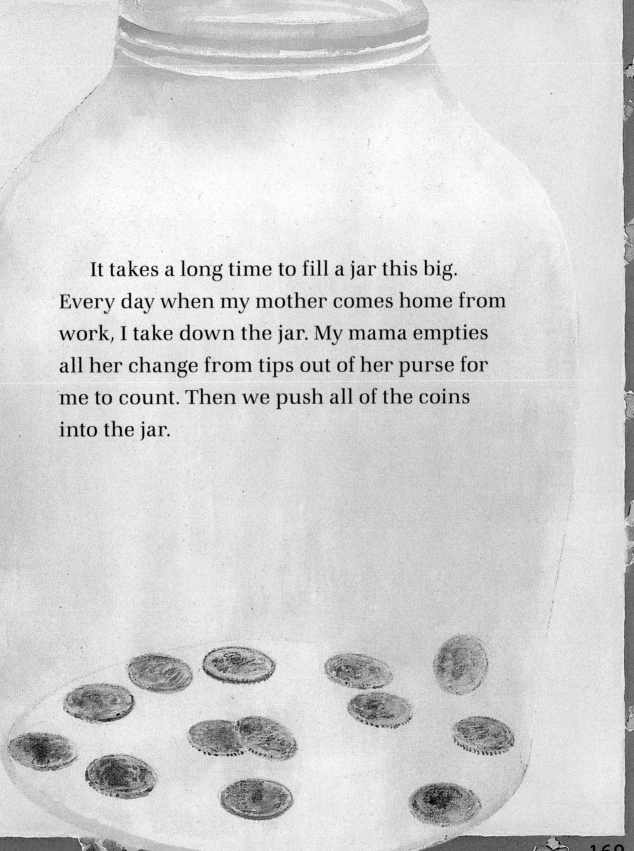

It takes a long time to fill a jar this big. Every day when my mother comes home from work, I take down the jar. My mama empties all her change from tips out of her purse for me to count. Then we push all of the coins into the jar.

Sometimes my mama is laughing
when she comes home from work.
Sometimes she's so tired she falls asleep
while I count the money out into piles.
Some days she has lots of tips. Some
days she has only a little. Then she looks
worried. But each evening every single
shiny coin goes into the jar.

We sit in the kitchen to count the tips. Usually Grandma sits with us too. While we count, she likes to hum. Often she has money in her old leather wallet for us. Whenever she gets a good bargain on tomatoes or bananas or something she buys, she puts by the savings and they go into the jar.

When we can't get a single other coin into the jar, we are going to take out all the money and go and buy a chair.

Yes, a chair. A wonderful, beautiful, fat, soft armchair. We will get one covered in velvet with roses all over it. We are going to get the best chair in the whole world.

That is because our old chairs burned up. There was a big fire in our other house. All our chairs burned. So did our sofa and so did everything else. That wasn't such a long time ago.

My mother and I were coming home from buying new shoes. I had new sandals. She had new pumps. We were walking to our house from the bus. We were looking at everyone's tulips. She was saying she liked red tulips and I was saying I liked yellow ones. Then we came to our block.

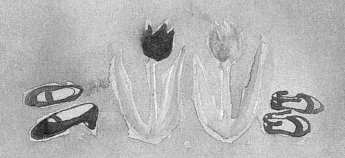

Right outside our house stood two big fire engines. I could see lots of smoke. Tall orange flames came out of the roof. All the neighbors stood in a bunch across the street. Mama grabbed my hand and we ran. My Uncle Sandy saw us and ran to us. Mama yelled, "Where's Mother?" I yelled, "Where's my grandma?" My Aunt Ida waved and shouted, "She's here, she's here. She's O.K. Don't worry."

Grandma was all right. Our cat was
safe too, though it took a while to find her.
But everything else in our whole house
was spoiled.

What was left of the house was turned to charcoal and ashes.

We went to stay with my mother's sister Aunt Ida and Uncle Sandy. Then we were able to move into the apartment downstairs. We painted the walls yellow. The floors were all shiny. But the rooms were very empty.

The first day we moved in, the neighbors brought pizza and cake and ice cream. And they brought a lot of other things too.

The family across the street brought a table and three kitchen chairs. The very old man next door gave us a bed from when his children were little.

My other grandpa brought us his beautiful
rug. My mother's other sister, Sally, had made us
red and white curtains. Mama's boss, Josephine,
brought pots and pans, silverware and dishes.
My cousin brought me her own stuffed bear.

Everyone clapped when my grandma made
a speech. "You are all the kindest people," she
said, "and we thank you very, very much. It's
lucky we're young and can start all over."

That was last year, but we still have no sofa and no big chairs. When Mama comes home, her feet hurt. "There's no good place for me to take a load off my feet," she says. When Grandma wants to sit back and hum and cut up potatoes, she has to get as comfortable as she can on a hard kitchen chair.

So that is how come Mama brought home the biggest jar she could find at the diner and all the coins started to go into the jar.

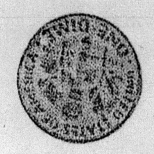

Now the jar is too heavy for me to lift down. Uncle Sandy gave me a quarter. He had to boost me up so I could put it in.

After supper Mama and Grandma and I stood in front of the jar. "Well, I never would have believed it, but I guess it's full," Mama said.

My mother brought home little paper
wrappers for the nickels and the dimes and
the quarters. I counted them all out and
wrapped them all up.

On my mother's day off, we took all the coins to the bank. The bank exchanged them for ten-dollar bills. Then we took the bus downtown to shop for our chair.

We shopped through four furniture stores. We tried out big chairs and smaller ones, high chairs and low chairs, soft chairs and harder ones. Grandma said she felt like Goldilocks in "The Three Bears" trying out all the chairs.

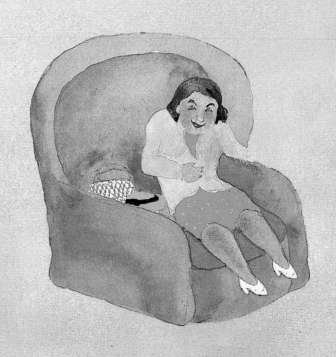

Finally we found the chair we were all dreaming of. And the money in the jar was enough to pay for it. We called Aunt Ida and Uncle Sandy. They came right down in their pickup truck to drive the chair home for us. They knew we couldn't wait for it to be delivered.

I tried out our chair in the back of the truck. Mama wouldn't let me sit there while we drove. But they let me sit in it while they carried it up to the door.

We set the chair right beside the window with the red and white curtains. Grandma and Mama and I all sat in it while Aunt Ida took our picture.

Now Grandma sits in it and talks with people going by in the daytime. Mama sits down and watches the news on TV when she comes home from her job. After supper, I sit with her and she can reach right up and turn out the light if I fall asleep in her lap.

Think Critically

R2.5
R3.2
W1.1

1 What problem do the characters in the story have? PLOT

2 Where do the family members get the money that goes into the jar? IMPORTANT DETAILS

3 Why do you think the family members try out so many chairs before they decide on one? DRAW CONCLUSIONS

4 How might the ending have been different if the characters had gone shopping for a chair after filling only a small jar with coins? SPECULATE

5 **WRITE** What lesson do you think the girl learned by saving money for so long? SHORT RESPONSE

CALIFORNIA STANDARDS
ENGLISH-LANGUAGE ARTS STANDARDS—Reading 2.5 Restate facts and details in the text to clarify and organize ideas; **Reading 3.2** Generate alternative endings to plots and identify the reason or reasons for, and the impact of, the alternatives; **Writing 1.1** Group related ideas and maintain a consistent focus.

Meet the Author and Illustrator
Vera B. Williams

Dear Readers,

The idea for "A Chair for My Mother" came from a wish I had as a child to be able to give my mother a marvelous gift. Like the family in the story, we did not have enough money to buy a new chair. I had a wonderful feeling that by writing this story, I could make that happen. Writing stories lets me change the past into something I like better.

Your friend,
Vera B. Williams

Saving Money

by Mary Firestone

Nonfiction

Saving Money

BY
MARY FIRESTONE

Putting money aside before you spend it helps you save. **Earnings** are money that you are paid or given. **Costs** are money you spend buying things. To save money, your earnings must be more than costs.

Dora is a second grader who wants to save her money. She spends only part of her earnings so she can save the rest.

Saving lets you buy more costly items without borrowing from others. Dora saves a little of her money each week. In time, she will save enough for a scooter.

Small amounts of money add up over time. If you put $2 in a jar each week, you will have $8 at the end of the month. After saving for a year, you would have more than $100.

You can keep your savings at a bank. Banks pay **interest**. Interest is a little bit of money the bank gives you for keeping money at their bank.

Dora writes what she brings to the bank in a passbook. When she wants to spend her money, the bank will give it back with interest.

Saving money is a good choice. Saving money
now will help you buy things you will need and want
later. Dora saved enough to buy her own scooter.
Saving money helps you plan for the future.

Connections

Comparing Texts

1 How do the characters save money in "A Chair for My Mother" and "Saving Money"?

2 What would you do with money you save?

3 What are some reasons people save money?

Phonics
R1.1

Read a Sentence

List five words in which *ou* or *ow* stand for the vowel sound in *cloud*. Trade lists with a partner. Then write a sentence using as many of the words as you can. Draw a picture for it. Read the sentence to your partner.

Fluency Practice R1.6

Read with Feeling

Take turns reading parts of the story with a partner.
Use your voices to show how the characters feel.
Practice until you agree that the pages sound right.

Writing W1.1

Write a Story

What would you save money to buy? Use a story map to plan a story. Then write your story.

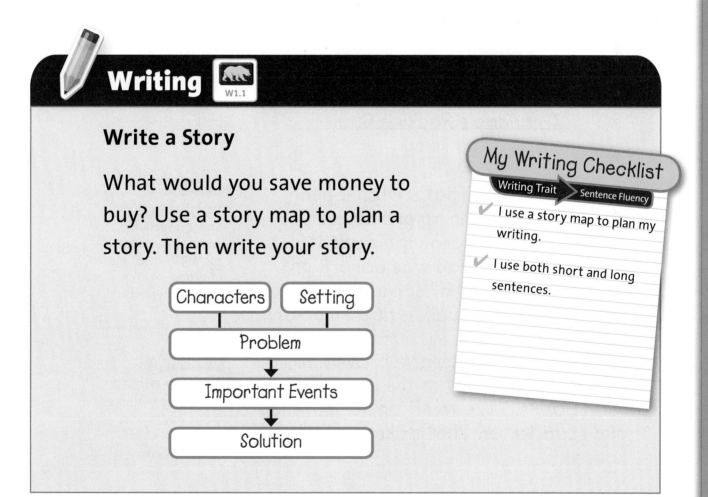

Characters Setting
Problem
Important Events
Solution

My Writing Checklist

Writing Trait → Sentence Fluency

✔ I use a story map to plan my writing.

✔ I use both short and long sentences.

Reading-Writing Connection

Description

A **description** tells how something looks, feels, smells, sounds, and tastes. In "A Chair for My Mother," the family buys a special chair. I wrote about my grandma's rocking chair.

Student Writing Model

<u>Grandma's Rocking Chair</u>
by Kaley

Creak! Creak! That's what I hear when I'm rocking in my grandma's rocking chair. My grandpa made it for her when my dad was born. Right now it has a coat of smooth, white paint. It has been painted other colors many times before. My dad says this is because it has been well loved. My grandma likes to sit in the chair and read books. I like to sit on her soft lap and read to her. That makes us both happy!

Writing Trait

WORD CHOICE
Choosing action verbs—for example, *rocking* instead of *sitting*—makes writing stronger and clearer.

Writing Trait

SENTENCE FLUENCY
Combining sentences is one way to help writing flow.

Here's how I write a description.

1. **I think about an item I want to describe. I think about the senses I can use to describe the item.**

2. **I use a graphic organizer. I write ideas I want to include in my description.**

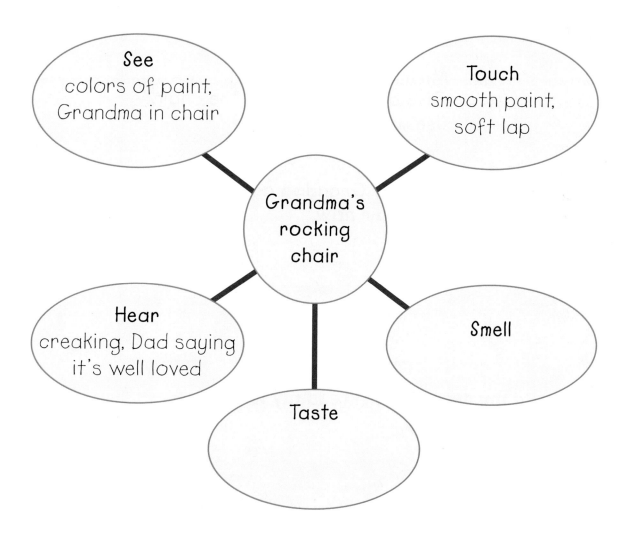

See
colors of paint,
Grandma in chair

Touch
smooth paint,
soft lap

Grandma's
rocking
chair

Smell

Hear
creaking, Dad saying
it's well loved

Taste

3. I look at my ideas, and I decide what to write about. I make my plan for writing.

Opening
Tell the main idea—the chair.
Use sound the chair makes.
Tell that Grandpa made the chair.

Middle
Give details. Describe the chair.
Use web.

Closing
Tell how Grandma and I use the chair now.

4. I write my description. I read my writing and make changes.

Here is a checklist I use when I write a description. You can use it when you write a description, too.

Checklist for Writing a Description

- ☐ My description has an interesting opening.

- ☐ Details give examples to add to the main idea.

- ☐ I create pictures in my readers' minds by telling what I see, hear, feel, smell, and taste.

- ☐ My description has a strong closing.

- ☐ I use action verbs to make my writing stronger and clearer.

- ☐ I combine sentences to help my writing flow.

Contents

Plot 204

Learn to compare the plots of two stories.

Vocabulary 206

Read, write, and learn the meanings of new words.

Serious Farm by Tim Egan 208

• Learn the features of a fantasy story.

• Use story structure to help you understand what you read.

Beyond Old MacDonald
by Charley Hoce
illustrated by Eugenie Fernandes 234

Read poems about life on a farm.

Connections 236

• Compare texts.

• Review phonics skills.

• Reread for fluency.

• Write a story.

Fantasy

SERIOUS FARM

TIM EGAN

Beyond Old MacDonald
Funny Poems from Down on the Farm

By Charley Hoce
Illustrated by Eugenie Fernandes

Poetry

Focus Skill

 Plot

The **plot** is what happens in a story. At the beginning, the characters have a problem. During the middle of the story, they try to find a solution. At the end, the characters usually solve the problem.

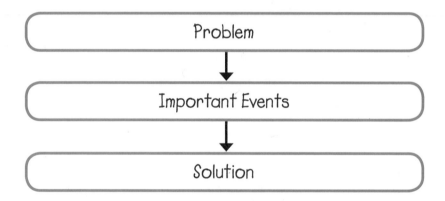

You can compare the plots of two stories. Think about these questions as you read.

- How are the characters' problems alike? How are they different?

- Do the characters solve their problems in the same way?

CALIFORNIA STANDARDS
ENGLISH-LANGUAGE ARTS STANDARDS—Reading 3.1 Compare and contrast plots, settings, and characters presented by different authors.

Read the story below again. How is Jill's problem like the characters' problem in "A Chair for My Mother"?

A Present for Mom

Mom's birthday was coming. Jill wanted to buy her flowers, but she had saved only $1.89. That wasn't enough for the flowers.

Then Jill had an idea. She would make some lemonade and set up a lemonade stand. After one day, Jill had made ten dollars. Now she could buy her mom flowers for her birthday.

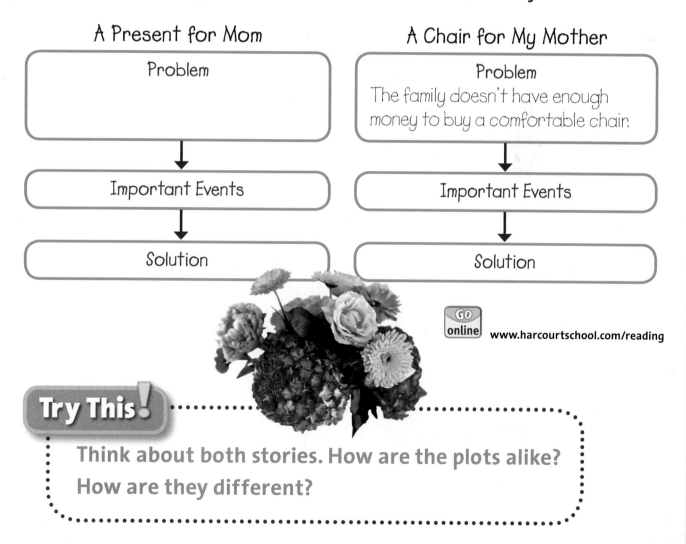

A Present for Mom

Problem

↓

Important Events

↓

Solution

A Chair for My Mother

Problem
The family doesn't have enough money to buy a comfortable chair.

↓

Important Events

↓

Solution

GO online www.harcourtschool.com/reading

Try This!

Think about both stories. How are the plots alike? How are they different?

Vocabulary

extremely

barely

admit

serious

hilarious

witty

Letter from Alyssa

Dear Mom and Dad,

Life on Aunt Abby's farm is different from life in the city. We get up when the rooster crows. This is **extremely** early. It's **barely** dawn! Then we feed the animals.

The first morning I was too tired to speak. I didn't **admit** I was tired, but I wasn't smiling or joking. Aunt Abby asked me why I was so **serious**. I told her that I'd be more cheerful once I woke up.

Then I said something Aunt Abby thought was **hilarious**. I asked if we could put the rooster in a dark closet. This way he wouldn't crow in the morning. She laughed and said she was glad I was waking up. I guess I was back to my **witty** self.

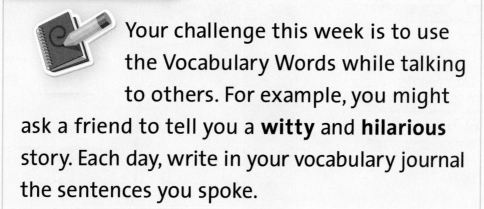

I'll write more later, but now we're going horseback riding.

Love,
Alyssa

 www.harcourtschool.com/reading

Word Champion

Your challenge this week is to use the Vocabulary Words while talking to others. For example, you might ask a friend to tell you a **witty** and **hilarious** story. Each day, write in your vocabulary journal the sentences you spoke.

SERIOUS FARM

Fantasy

Genre Study

A **fantasy** is a story that could not really happen. Look for

- made-up characters.
- a make-believe plot.

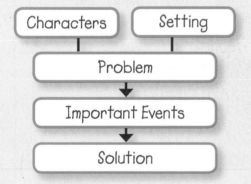

Characters | Setting
Problem
Important Events
Solution

R2.5

Comprehension Strategy

Use **story structure** to think about how characters solve their problem.

CALIFORNIA STANDARDS
ENGLISH-LANGUAGE ARTS STANDARDS—
Reading 2.5 Restate facts and details in the text to clarify and organize ideas.

SERIOUS
FARM

by
TIM EGAN

Farmer Fred never smiled much. He wasn't
a sad fellow, just very serious. "Farmin' is serious
business," he'd say. "Nothing funny about corn."

Now, because it was Farmer Fred's farm, all
the animals acted the way he did, so they were
very serious, too.

When he would say, "There's no humor in
tomatoes," they'd all agree.

The pigs, the cows, the horses, the chickens,
the rabbit, the sheep. All extremely serious.

211

One night, Edna, the cow, said, "We've got
to get Farmer Fred to laugh. I mean, it's okay
to be serious, but not all the time. We need
some laughter."

"Must admit," said Bernie, the goat, "I
wouldn't mind smilin' again."

He stretched his mouth and showed all his
teeth. It wasn't a very convincing smile. They all
decided they needed a plan to make the farm
more fun.

The next morning, as the sun came up, Edna was standing on the fence where Cormac, the rooster, usually stood.

She was barely able to keep her balance.

She tried to yell, "Cock-a-doodle-do," but since she was a cow, it didn't come out like that at all. It was the first time anyone had done anything funny in months, so it made all the animals laugh.

Farmer Fred just looked out the window and said, "You're not a rooster," and shut the window and went back to sleep.

"Wow," said Edna, "this is gonna be tougher than I thought."

That morning was serious as usual, with Farmer
Fred saying things like "Broccoli's no fun" and
"I never laugh at bell peppers."

"Okay," said Edna to the others, "let's try
another idea."

When Farmer Fred went to feed the pigs that
afternoon, they started barking like dogs. Everyone
thought it was hilarious but Farmer Fred.

"That's more weird than funny," he said as he walked away.

"All right," said Edna, "this isn't working. Let's try something new."

They sneaked into the house and took some clothes from Farmer Fred's closet and put them on. It wasn't as easy as it sounds.

That evening, as the moon lit up the field,
Bernie rang the doorbell. Farmer Fred came out
onto the porch and said, "What in the world?"
The animals were all dancing around in Farmer
Fred's clothes.

They were terrible dancers, which actually
made it funnier. But Farmer Fred just said,
"Better not get my clothes dirty."
He walked back inside without smiling.

For the next two weeks, the animals tried
everything they could to make Farmer Fred smile
a little, but nothing worked.

It got to be very discouraging.

One night, the animals met in the barn.

"Well, I don't know about you," said Edna, "but I can't take it anymore. I have to live somewhere more fun than this. I'm leaving."

They all agreed with Edna and packed up
their stuff, which wasn't much, and headed
out into the night.

The next morning, there was no sound of a
rooster or even a cow. Farmer Fred looked outside
and saw that all the animals were gone.

"Oh no," he said, "all the animals are gone."

Farmer Fred became sad immediately. Now,
it was one thing to be serious, but it was another
thing to be sad.

Farmer Fred didn't like the feeling at all.

He got into his truck and drove down the road in search of his friends.

He went about four miles, but there was no sign of them anywhere. Then he heard some laughter in the distance.

He followed the sound and saw the animals walking through the woods.

He got out of his truck, walked into the forest, and asked, "What's going on here?"

"We couldn't stand it," said Edna. "We've tried to cheer you up, but nothing's worked, so we're running away. Well, walking away."

The other animals nodded in agreement.

"Well, that's no way to solve a problem," said Farmer Fred. "You don't just leave. I mean, sure, I'm serious, but that doesn't mean you have to be. And, besides, we're family. I take care of you. I need you.

"Not to mention that you're safe on the farm. You'd probably be eaten by lions in a day or two out here in the woods."

The animals thought about this for a moment.

As they whispered to one another about the lion issue, Farmer Fred mumbled, "Cows and chickens runnin' wild in the woods, heh, heh."

Edna turned quickly and said, "What was that?"

"I think he laughed a little," said Bernie.

"Yes," said a chicken, "I heard it. It wasn't much, but he did laugh."

"Well," said Edna, "in that case, you're witty enough for us, Farmer Fred. And we care about you, too. I guess we can go back to the farm."

The other animals nodded their heads and said things like "I agree" and "Good idea" and "Let's go back."

They hopped onto the truck and Farmer Fred drove them home.

From that day forward, they were able to make Farmer Fred laugh a little more, especially by bringing up the idea of cows and chickens running wild, although he still doesn't see anything funny about corn.

Think Critically

R2.5
W1.1
W2.1b

1 What problem do the animals in the story have? 🌀 PLOT

2 Why do the animals leave the farm? IMPORTANT DETAILS

3 Why do you think Farmer Fred feels sad when he sees that the animals are gone? DRAW CONCLUSIONS

4 What did Farmer Fred say or do that might have made the animals want to return home? How do you know? MAKE INFERENCES

5 **WRITE** How can you tell that Farmer Brown cares a lot about the animals? Use examples from the story to explain your answer. ✏️ SHORT RESPONSE

CALIFORNIA STANDARDS
ENGLISH-LANGUAGE ARTS STANDARDS—Reading 2.5 Restate facts and details in the text to clarify and organize ideas; **Writing 1.1** Group related ideas and maintain a consistent focus; **Writing 2.1b** Describe the setting, characters, objects, and events in detail.

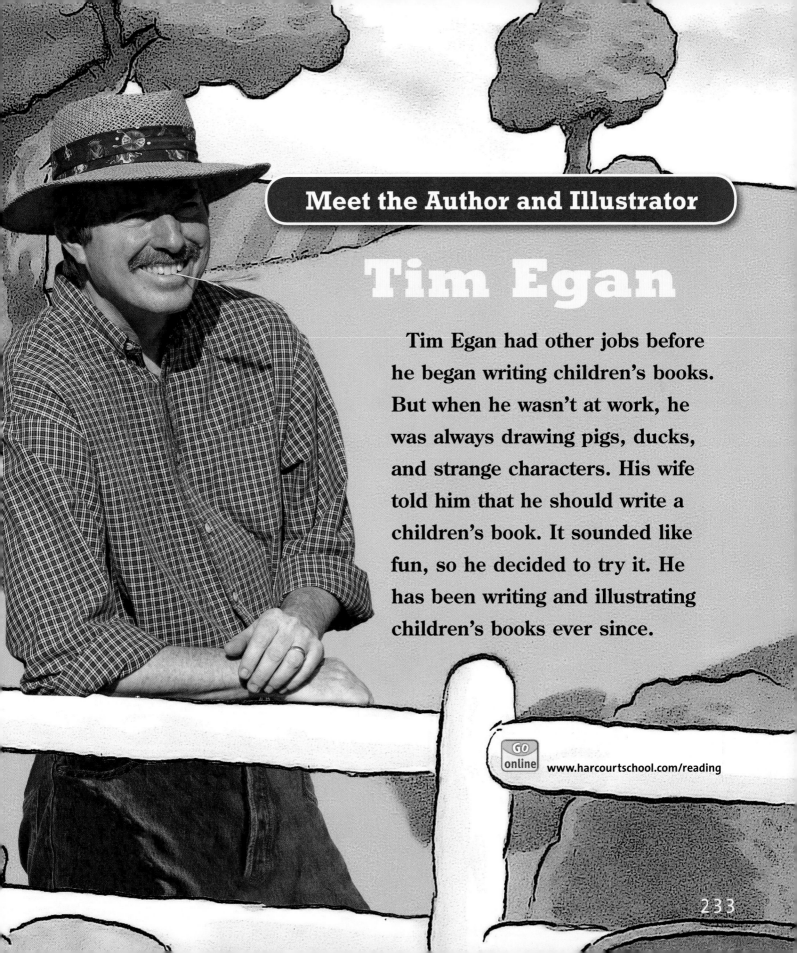

Meet the Author and Illustrator

Tim Egan

Tim Egan had other jobs before he began writing children's books. But when he wasn't at work, he was always drawing pigs, ducks, and strange characters. His wife told him that he should write a children's book. It sounded like fun, so he decided to try it. He has been writing and illustrating children's books ever since.

GO online www.harcourtschool.com/reading

233

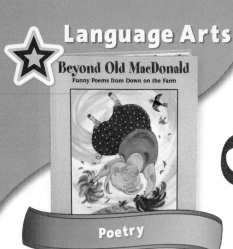

Beyond Old MacDonald
Funny Poems from Down on the Farm

Poetry

Beyond Old MacDonald

poems by Charley Hoce
illustrated by Eugenie Fernandes

Mischievous Goat

The baby goat was scolded
For the mischievous things he did.
But no one got too angry
After all, he's just a kid.

234

When My Cow Goes Dancing

When my cow goes dancing
At the weekly fashion ball,
She always wears a muumuu
Since it makes her calves look small.

Farm Family

My mother patches all my jeans
My grandma makes my clothes
But when he's on a tractor
My dad's the one who sows.

235

Connections

Comparing Texts

1 What do the cows do in "Serious Farm" and "When My Cow Goes Dancing"?

2 What kinds of things make you laugh?

3 How are the animals in "Serious Farm" different from real animals?

Phonics

Make Picture Cards

Write words in which the letters *or, ore,* or *our* stand for the vowel sound in *fork.* Draw a picture for each. Share your words with a partner.

CALIFORNIA STANDARDS
ENGLISH-LANGUAGE ARTS STANDARDS—Reading 1.1 Recognize and use knowledge of spelling patterns (e.g., diphthongs, special vowel spellings) when reading; **Reading 1.6** Read aloud fluently and accurately and with appropriate intonation and expression; **Reading 3.1** Compare and contrast plots, settings, and characters presented by different authors; **Writing 1.1** Group related ideas and maintain a consistent focus.

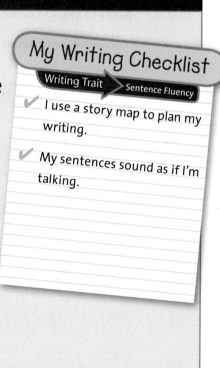

Fluency Practice

R1.6

Readers' Theater

Work with a group to read "Serious Farm" as Readers' Theater. Think about how the characters should sound. Make the sounds that the animals make!

Writing

W1.1

Write a Story

Write a story about making someone laugh. Plan what will happen in the beginning, middle, and end. Think about what problem your characters will solve. Then write the story.

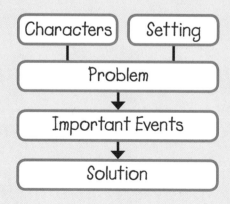

My Writing Checklist

Writing Trait → Sentence Fluency

✔ I use a story map to plan my writing.

✔ My sentences sound as if I'm talking.

Contents

Words with *oo, ew, ue, ui,* and *ou* 240

Learn to read words with *oo, ew, ue, ui,* and *ou.*

Vocabulary 242

Read, write, and learn the meanings of new words.

The Bee by Sabrina Crewe 244

• Learn the features of nonfiction.

• Think about the most important ideas by summarizing.

California Bee Business by Dimarie Santiago 274

Read about why bees are important in California.

Connections 276

• Compare texts.

• Review phonics skills.

• Reread for fluency.

• Write a description.

Lesson 23

Nonfiction

LIFE CYCLES

The
Bee

California
Bee
Business
by Dimarie Santiago

Nonfiction

Phonics Skill

Words with *oo*, *ew*, *ue*, *ui*, *ou*

The letters *oo*, *ew*, *ue*, *ui*, and *ou* can stand for the same sound. Read the words below.

spoon

dew

glue

fruit

soup

Do you hear the same vowel sound in each word?

CALIFORNIA STANDARDS
ENGLISH-LANGUAGE ARTS STANDARDS—Reading 1.1 Recognize and use knowledge of spelling patterns (e.g., diphthongs, special vowel spellings) when reading.

Read each word on the left. Tell which word on the right has the same sound.

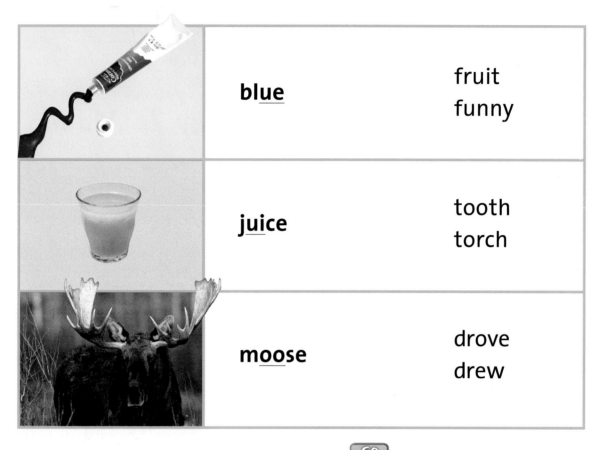

	bl<u>ue</u>	fruit funny
	j<u>ui</u>ce	tooth torch
	m<u>oo</u>se	drove drew

GO online www.harcourtschool.com/reading

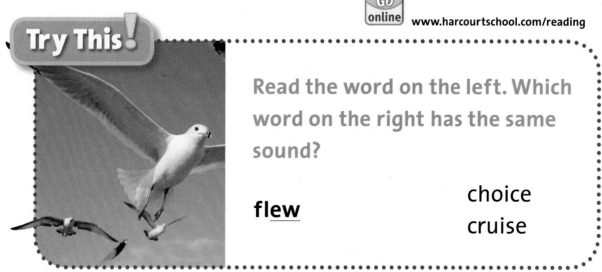

Try This!

Read the word on the left. Which word on the right has the same sound?

fl<u>ew</u>

choice
cruise

pattern

sealed

carefully

attack

crowd

disappear

How Honey Is Made

Honey drizzled in a **pattern** on toast is a sweet treat to eat! How does honey get into a **sealed** jar?

Bees make honey in their hives. Beekeepers are people who care for and raise bees. They raise bees **carefully** to keep them healthy.

Beekeepers keep their bees in special boxes. These boxes become the bees' home, or hive. The bees raise their young and make honey there. The honey is the bees' food.

Beekeepers must be careful when they gather honey from a hive. Most bees can sting. They **attack** anyone or anything that disturbs their hive. Many beekeepers wear a bee suit. A bee suit helps keep a beekeeper safe when angry bees **crowd** around him or her. The bee suit doesn't make the bees **disappear**. It just makes it hard for them to sting the person.

GO online www.harcourtschool.com/reading

Word Scribe

This week your task is to use the Vocabulary Words in your writing. For example, you might write a note to your teacher that says "Last night I saw a star **pattern** in the sky." At the end of each day, write in your vocabulary journal the sentences that had Vocabulary Words.

The
Bee

Nonfiction

Genre Study

Nonfiction gives information about the world. Look for

- graphic aids, such as diagrams, that give more facts.

- paragraphs with main ideas and details.

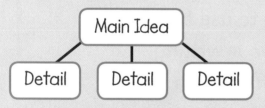

R2.5

Comprehension Strategy

Summarize a selection to help you think about the most important ideas.

by Sabrina Crewe

CALIFORNIA STANDARDS
ENGLISH-LANGUAGE ARTS STANDARDS—
Reading 2.5 Restate facts and details in the text to clarify and organize ideas.

244

The Bee

What is inside the tree?

There is a beehive inside the tree trunk. The hive is made of several parts called combs. Thousands of bees live together in one hive.

The bees are working together.

The bees that look after the hive are female bees called workers. The worker bees make wax inside their bodies. They use the wax to build cells for the combs.

Look at this comb.

All the cells have six sides.

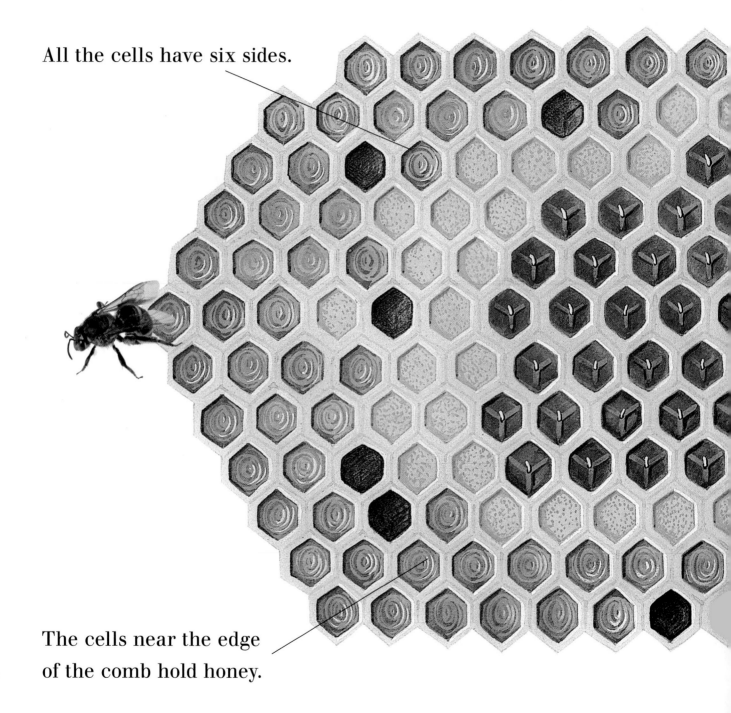

The cells near the edge
of the comb hold honey.

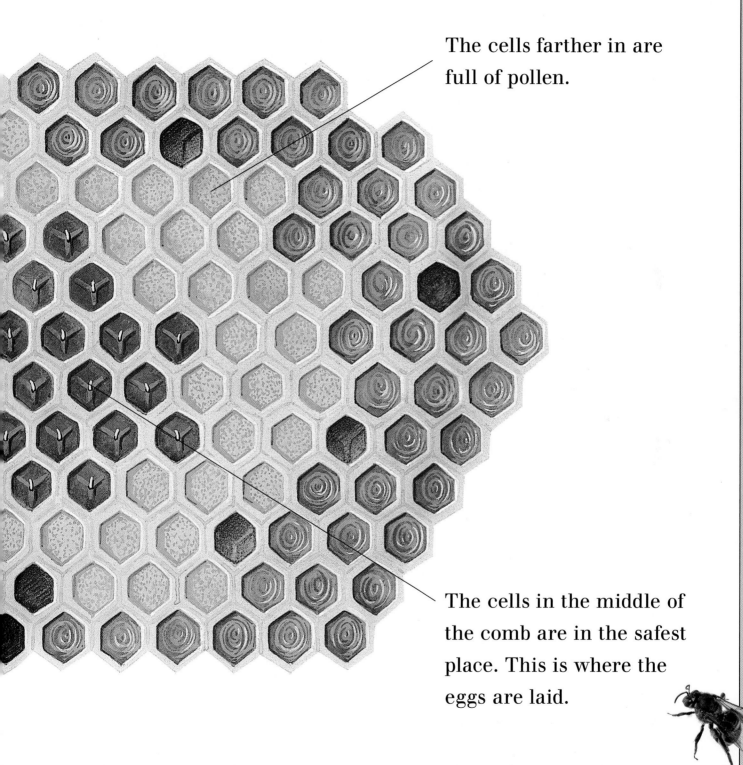

The cells farther in are full of pollen.

The cells in the middle of the comb are in the safest place. This is where the eggs are laid.

The queen bee is laying an egg.

Only one bee in the hive can lay eggs. She is called the queen bee, and she is bigger than the worker bees. The workers feed her and take good care of her. They crowd around the queen bee when she lays her eggs.

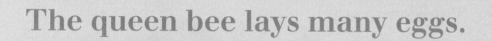

The queen bee lays many eggs.

The queen bee can lay hundreds of eggs in a day. She lays each one in its own cell. The eggs are very small.

Actual size of eggs

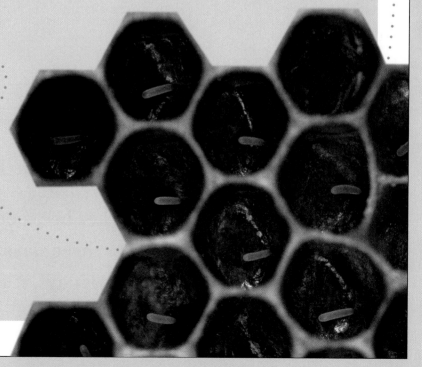

The larva has come out of its egg.

After three days, the larvae that are inside the eggs hatch. A larva comes out of each egg. The larvae stay inside their cells. They are looked after by worker bees.

The larva is being fed.

The worker bee feeds the larva to make it grow. For the first three days, the larva eats royal jelly. For the next three days, it feeds on pollen and honey.

The bees have covered the cells.

After six days, the larvae have grown enough to fill their cells. The cells are sealed with wax by worker bees. Now the larvae turn into pupae.

The pupa is turning into a bee.

The pupa rests in its cell. Many changes are taking place inside the pupa. After 12 days, the pupa will become a bee.

The bee is coming out.

The bee chews through the wax. At first, the bee is very soft, and its new wings are wet. Older workers share their nectar with young bees until they are ready to find their own food.

The new bee starts to work.

The bee's first job is to clean empty cells. It climbs into the cells and cleans them carefully. The clean cells can be used for new eggs.

Worker bees look after drones.

Young workers feed the male bees when they come out of their cells. Male bees are called drones. Drones are bigger than worker bees, and they have larger eyes. They do not work at all in the hive.

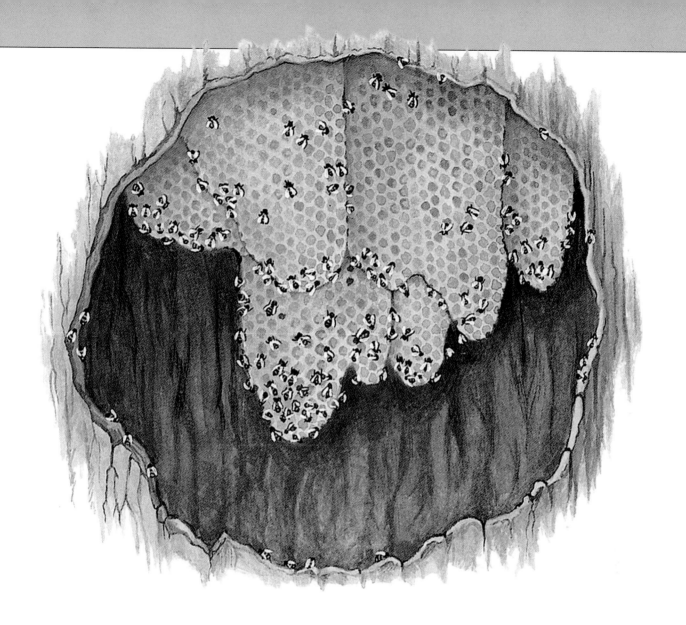

The bees are guarding the hive.

When worker bees are two weeks old, they start work around the edge of the hive. They clean and fix the hive, and watch out for enemies. The bees will sting any enemies who attack the hive.

The bee flies out of the hive.

Bees make their first flight when they are three weeks old. They fly around their hive to learn its shape and where it is. Then they are ready to search for food.

The bee visits a flower.

Bees suck nectar from flowers with their proboscis. They carry the nectar in a special stomach. The bee must get nectar from many flowers before its stomach is full.

The bee is carrying pollen.

Pollen from flowers sticks to the bee's body while it is getting nectar. The bee packs the pollen onto the pollen baskets on its back legs. Then it carries the pollen back to its hive.

The bees bring food for the hive.

The bees find cells to store their pollen. Then they feed some nectar to young workers and drones. The nectar that is left over is given to other workers, who turn it into honey. The honey is stored in cells, too.

The bee is dancing.

The bee with the pollen is showing the other bees where it found its nectar. The dance shows the other bees which way to go. The bee dances very fast in a circle if the flowers are close. If the flowers are far away, it slowly makes a pattern like an 8.

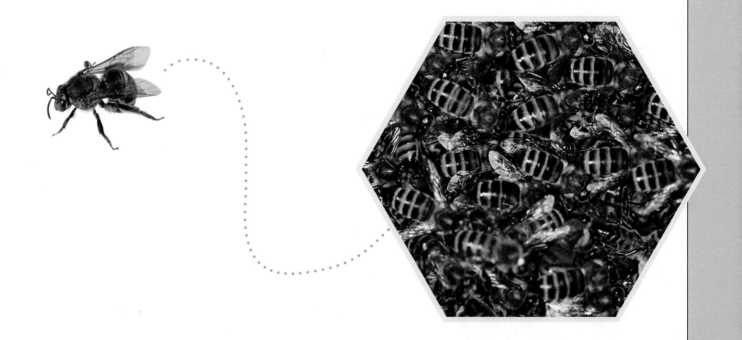

The hive is getting crowded.

The queen bee has laid many eggs. The hive is full of bees. It is time for some of the bees to leave.

The bees are swarming.

Some of the bees are leaving their hive in a swarm. The queen bee goes with them. The swarm gathers on a branch while a few bees look for a good place to make a new hive.

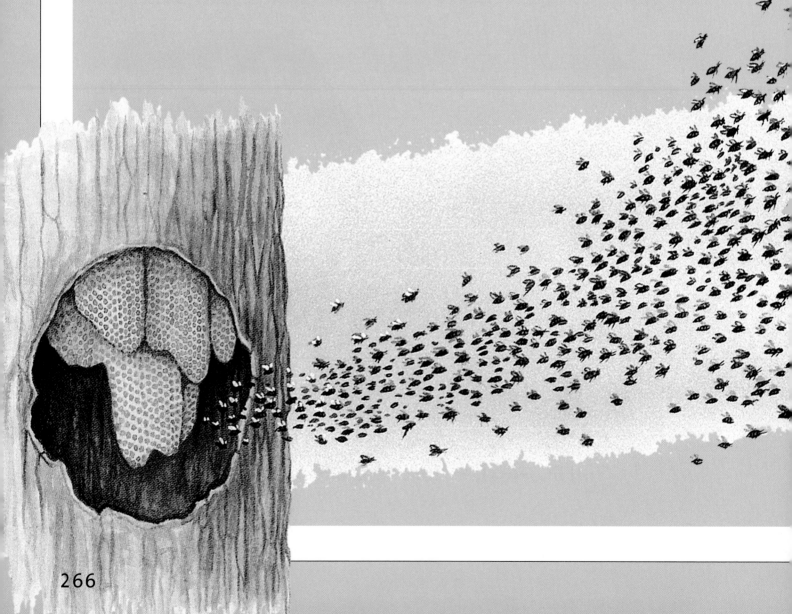

A new queen takes over.

A new queen bee has been born in the old hive. She starts laying eggs.

The honey cells are full.

By the end of the summer, the bees have filled the hive with honey. They start to cover the honey cells with wax. There won't be any nectar in the fall and the winter. The bees will live on the honey stored in the honey cells.

268

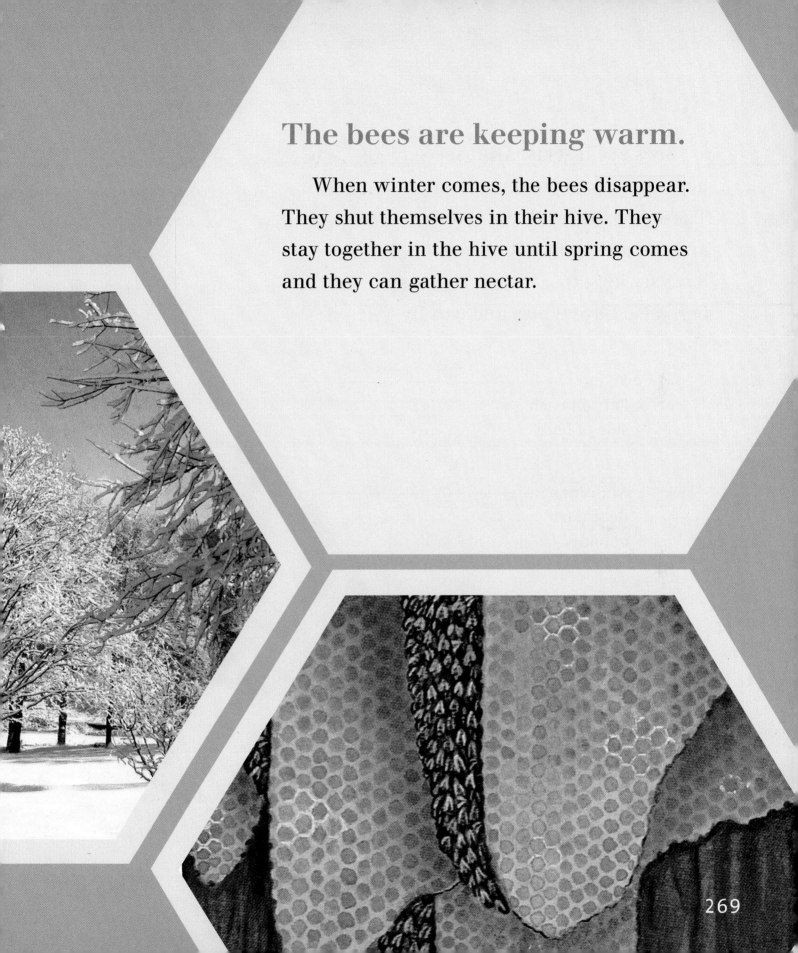

The bees are keeping warm.

When winter comes, the bees disappear. They shut themselves in their hive. They stay together in the hive until spring comes and they can gather nectar.

269

Parts of a Bee

Bees are insects. All insects have three parts to their body. These are the head, the thorax, and the abdomen. All insects have six legs, too. Insects such as bees also have wings and can fly.

Wings
Pair on each
side of body

Abdomen
Rear part
of body

Pollen baskets
Long hairs on legs
to carry pollen

Stinger
Sharp point used
to fight enemies

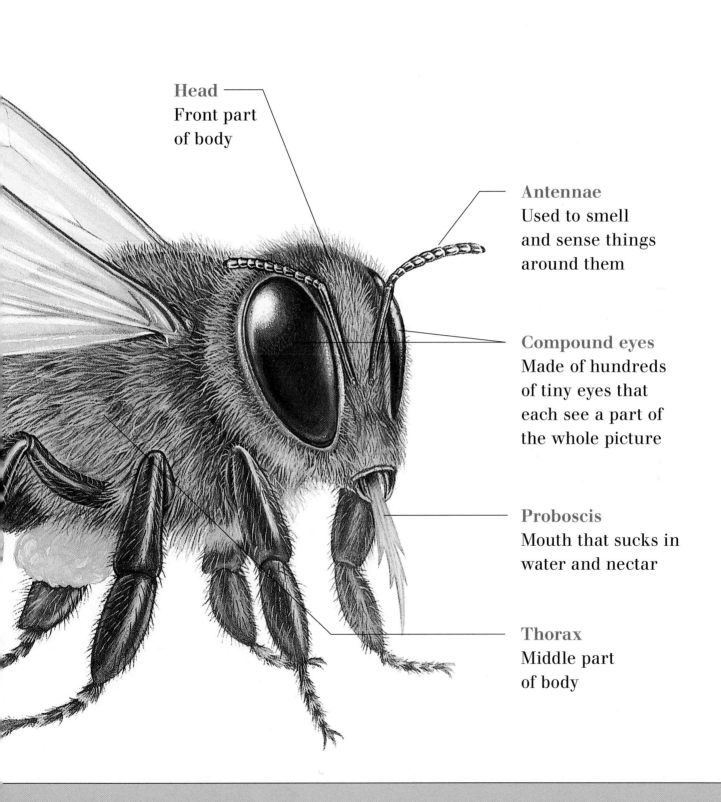

Head
Front part
of body

Antennae
Used to smell
and sense things
around them

Compound eyes
Made of hundreds
of tiny eyes that
each see a part of
the whole picture

Proboscis
Mouth that sucks in
water and nectar

Thorax
Middle part
of body

Think Critically

R2.5
R2.7
W1.1
W2.1b

1 Look at the diagram on pages 270–271. What is the thorax? GRAPHIC AIDS

2 What are the four stages in the life cycle of a bee? DRAW CONCLUSIONS

3 What do worker bees build with the wax they make? IMPORTANT DETAILS

4 Why do you think there can only be one queen in each hive? MAKE INFERENCES

5 **WRITE** Which type of bee is the busiest bee in the hive? Use examples from the selection to explain. SHORT RESPONSE

CALIFORNIA STANDARDS
ENGLISH-LANGUAGE ARTS STANDARDS—Reading 2.5 Restate facts and details in the text to clarify and organize ideas; **Reading 2.7** Interpret information from diagrams, charts, and graphs; **Writing 1.1** Group related ideas and maintain a consistent focus; **Writing 2.1b** Describe the setting, characters, objects, and events in detail.

Meet the Author
Sabrina Crewe

Sabrina Crewe has been writing stories and poems since she was a young girl. Many of her family members are writers, so she wanted to become a writer, too.

Sabrina Crewe has written more than 40 books for children. Many of her books are about animals. Some other books that she has written are about events that happened in the United States long ago.

GO online www.harcourtschool.com/reading

Nonfiction

California

Bee Business

by Dimarie Santiago

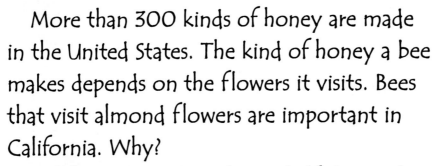

More than 300 kinds of honey are made in the United States. The kind of honey a bee makes depends on the flowers it visits. Bees that visit almond flowers are important in California. Why?

California produces almost half the world's almonds. When bees visit almond flowers, they spread the flowers' pollen that makes almonds grow. It takes almost a million hives of bees to keep California's almonds growing!

Bees are attracted to the fragrant flowers on almond trees.

When caring for a hive, beekeepers use smoke to calm the bees.

California is one of the top producers of honey in the nation. In a recent year, California produced about 15 million pounds of honey! That's almost enough for every person in California to have half a pound of honey. How much honey do you eat?

Connections

Comparing Texts

1 What do "The Bee" and "California Bee Business" tell you about how flowers help bees make honey?

2 What else would you like to know about bees?

3 In what places might bees be unable to make honey?

Phonics

Word Clues

List words in which the letters *oo, ew, ue, ui,* or *ou* stand for the vowel sound in *tooth*. Write clues for your words. Take turns with a partner to guess each other's words.

> This word names apples, oranges, and bananas.

> fr<u>ui</u>t

CALIFORNIA STANDARDS
ENGLISH-LANGUAGE ARTS STANDARDS—Reading 1.1 Recognize and use knowledge of spelling patterns (e.g., diphthongs, special vowel spellings) when reading; **Reading 1.6** Read aloud fluently and accurately and with appropriate intonation and expression; *(continued)*

Fluency Practice

R1.6

Partner Reading

Read the selection again with a partner. Take turns reading one or two pages at a time. Try to read at a pace that sounds like you are talking to a friend.

Writing

W1.1

Make a Diagram

Find information about an animal that interests you. Write about the animal. Use a chart to plan your main idea and details. Then make a diagram to show the parts of the animal.

My Writing Checklist

Writing Trait ➤ Word Choice

✔ My writing has a main idea and supporting details.

✔ I use lively verbs.

✔ My diagram shows the parts of my animal.

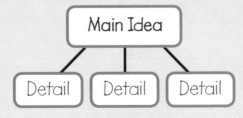

```
        ┌──────────┐
        │ Main Idea │
        └──────────┘
       ╱      │      ╲
┌────────┐┌────────┐┌────────┐
│ Detail ││ Detail ││ Detail │
└────────┘└────────┘└────────┘
```

Reading 2.5 Restate facts and details in the text to clarify and organize ideas; **Writing 1.1** Group related ideas and maintain a consistent focus.

277

Contents

Use Graphic Aids 280

Learn to use graphic aids to help you understand
what you read.

Vocabulary 282

Read, write, and learn the meanings of new words.

Watching in the Wild by Charnan Simon 284

• Learn the features of nonfiction.

• Summarize a selection to understand the main ideas.

Chimp Computer Whiz from *Ask* 298

Read about chimpanzees that use a computer.

Connections 300

• Compare texts.

• Review phonics skills.

• Reread for fluency.

• Write about an event.

Lesson 24

Nonfiction

WATCHING IN THE WILD

by Charnan Simon

Chimp Computer Whiz

Magazine Article

279

Use Graphic Aids

Nonfiction often uses **graphic aids** to help explain information quickly. Some examples of graphic aids are diagrams, charts, maps, and graphs.

- A diagram is a drawing with labels. It shows the parts of something or how something works.

- A chart has rows, columns, and headings.

- A map is a picture that shows where places are.

- A graph is a drawing that gives information about the amounts of things.

Diagram of a Plant

flower

stem

leaves

roots

CALIFORNIA STANDARDS
ENGLISH-LANGUAGE ARTS STANDARDS—Reading 2.7 Interpret
information from diagrams, charts, and graphs.

Read the passage. Look at the diagram. Tell which information in the passage is made clear in the diagram.

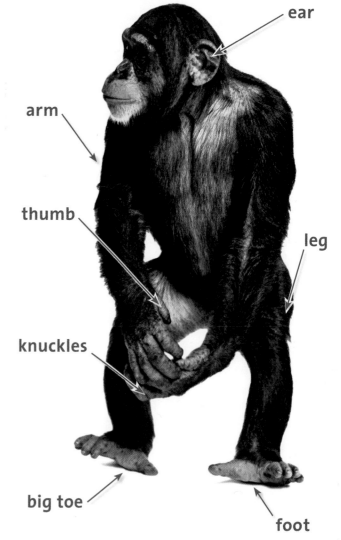

ear

arm

thumb

leg

knuckles

big toe

foot

A chimpanzee spends much of its time in trees. Its thumbs and big toes help it grab things. Its long arms are useful for swinging through trees. When a chimpanzee walks, it usually leans on its knuckles and walks on all fours.

www.harcourtschool.com/reading

Try This!

Look back at the diagram. What does it explain?

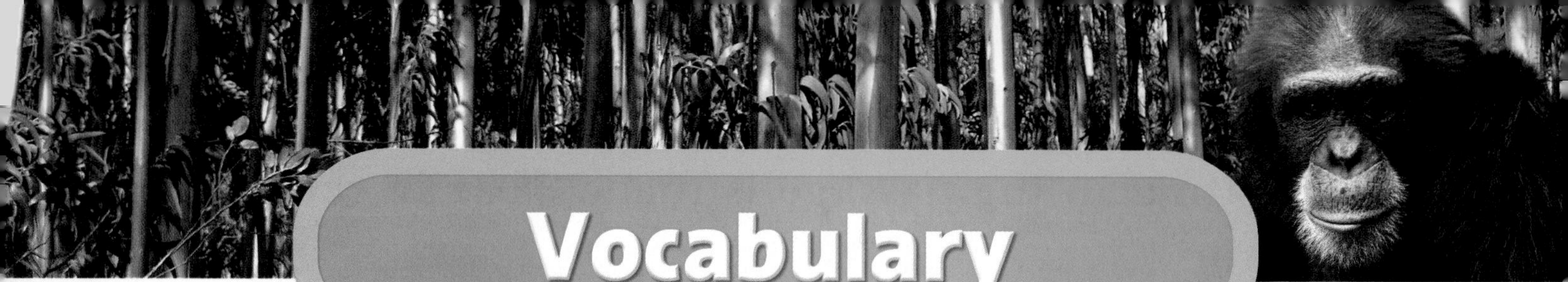

Vocabulary

Build Robust Vocabulary

- blended
- cradled
- raggedy
- personalities
- distance
- crumpled

Zoe's Photos

Zoe wanted to take pictures of deer, but often it was hard to see them. The deer **blended** in with the trees around them. Zoe and her dad found a good place to watch for deer.

While they waited for the deer to appear, Zoe **cradled** her camera in her lap. When they came, she took lots of pictures. Zoe gave the deer names.

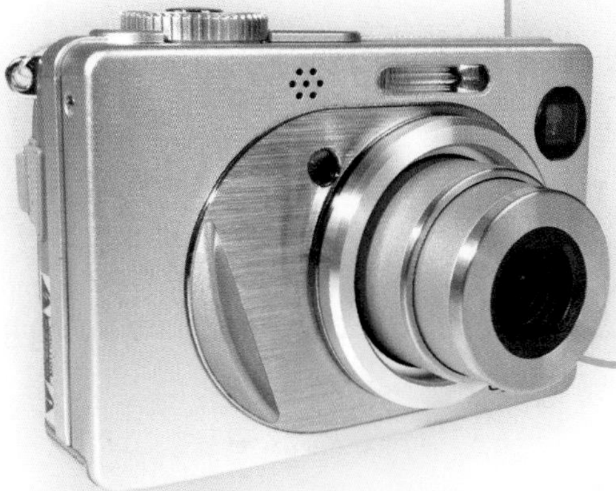

Zoe named one deer Rags. He was shedding his thick fur and looked **raggedy**. Zoe named other deer by their **personalities**. She named a curious deer Nosy. One deer reminded Zoe of her shy cousin. Zoe named him Bashful. He always stayed at a **distance**.

After an hour of watching deer, Zoe and her dad stood up. Their clothes were all **crumpled**. Zoe wondered what the deer would name her and her dad!

 www.harcourtschool.com/reading

Word Detective

Where else can you find the Vocabulary Words? Look on billboards and signs around town. Listen to announcements and songs. When you see or hear one of the words, write it in your vocabulary journal and tell where you found it.

WATCHING IN THE WILD
by Charnan Simon

Nonfiction

Genre Study

Nonfiction gives information about the world. Look for

- headings that tell what each section is about.
- graphic aids such as time lines.

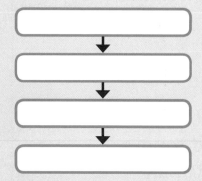

R2.5

Comprehension Strategy

Summarize a selection to understand the main ideas.

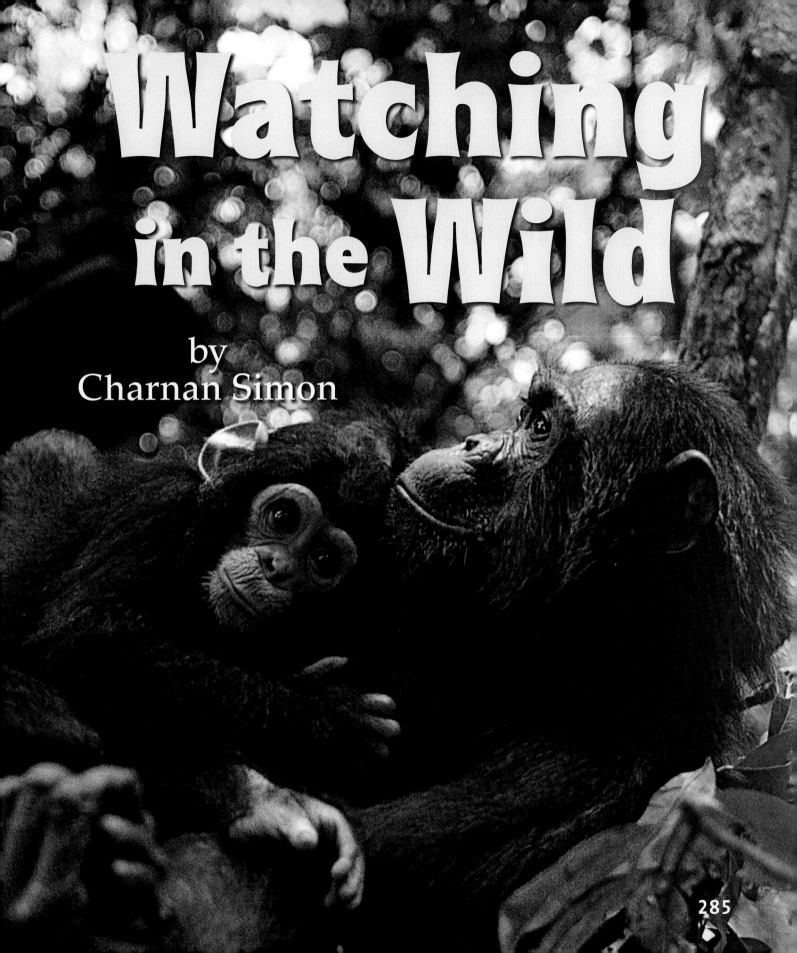

Watching in the Wild

by Charnan Simon

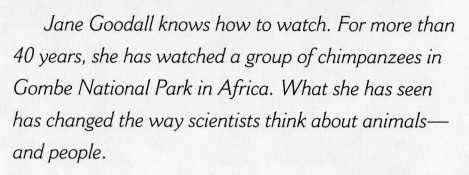

Jane Goodall knows how to watch. For more than 40 years, she has watched a group of chimpanzees in Gombe National Park in Africa. What she has seen has changed the way scientists think about animals— and people.

Travels to Africa

Jane was 26 years old when she first went to Gombe. It was 1960, and no one had ever studied chimpanzees in the wild. Jane's plan was simple. She would travel to Africa and find some chimpanzees. Then she would sit quietly and watch them go about their lives.

◀ **Jane Goodall**

286

Gombe
National
Park ▶

Watching and Learning

When she arrived at Gombe, Jane could hear chimpanzees calling to each other across the valleys. She found half-eaten fruits under trees where they had fed. But she didn't see the chimpanzees themselves. They were shy! Whenever Jane came close, they ran away.

287

▲ **Chimpanzees**

Jane was discouraged. But she didn't give up. If the chimpanzees didn't want her to come close, she would watch them from a distance. Every day she woke up before dawn. She put on clothes that blended in with the jungle and climbed to the top of a high, rocky ledge. Using binoculars, she sat and looked at chimpanzees—hour after hour after hour.

Other people might have been bored. Not Jane! She loved watching the chimpanzees feeding in fig trees and drinking from streams.

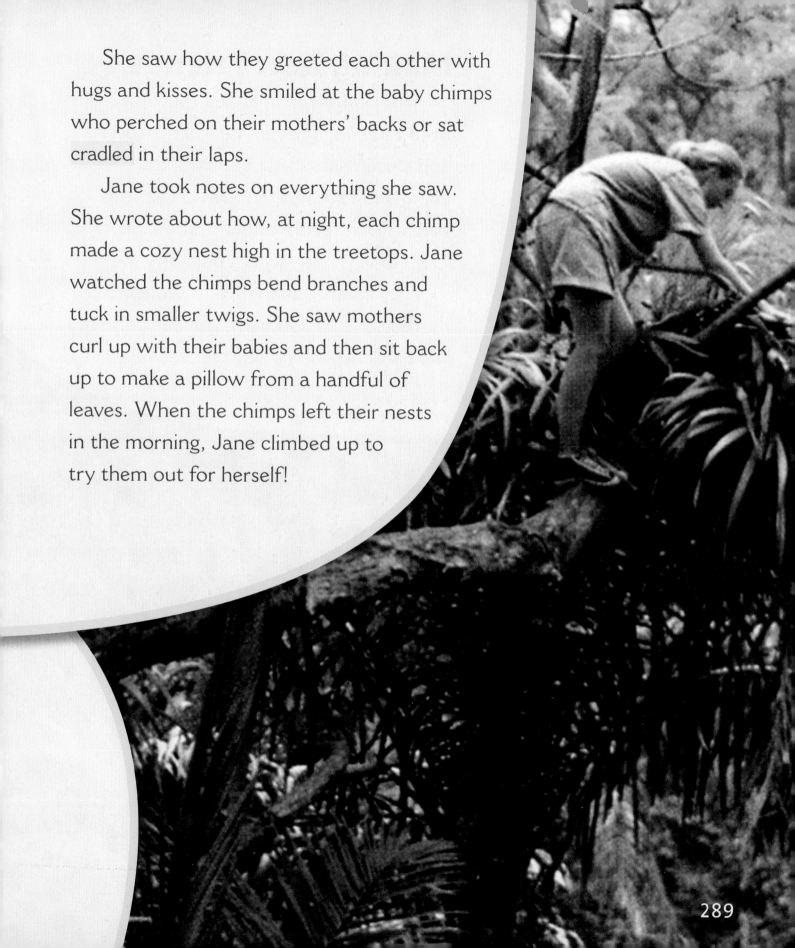

She saw how they greeted each other with hugs and kisses. She smiled at the baby chimps who perched on their mothers' backs or sat cradled in their laps.

Jane took notes on everything she saw. She wrote about how, at night, each chimp made a cozy nest high in the treetops. Jane watched the chimps bend branches and tuck in smaller twigs. She saw mothers curl up with their babies and then sit back up to make a pillow from a handful of leaves. When the chimps left their nests in the morning, Jane climbed up to try them out for herself!

Making New Friends

Slowly, the chimpanzees became used to Jane. They let her come closer and closer. Jane began naming the chimps she recognized. David Greybeard had a silvery beard and a calm manner. Old Flo was ugly, with a big nose and raggedy ears—but she was a wonderful mother. Mr. McGregor reminded Jane of the gardener in *The Tale of Peter Rabbit*.

▲ **A chimpanzee and her baby**

At the time, scientists thought that animals being studied should be given numbers, not names. But Jane didn't agree. She saw that the chimpanzees had real personalities. It made sense to give them real names. Today, many scientists name the animals they study in the wild.

Observing Tool Use

One day Jane saw something really exciting. David Greybeard was sitting by a red-earth termite mound. He poked a long grass stem into a hole in the mound. Then he pulled the stem out and ate the crunchy termites that clung to it.

◄ Flo fishes for termites while her young son watches and learns.

Jane was amazed. David Greybeard was
using the grass stem as a tool! Until then, scientists
thought that only people used tools. Jane saw the
chimps using other tools, too. Once, a big brother
chimp grabbed a handful of leaves to wipe his little
brother's messy nose. Many times, chimps used
crumpled leaves as sponges to soak up water to
drink from hollow logs.

Jane Goodall's Time Line

1930   1940   1950   1960

1934
Jane is born.

1942
Jane is given a book about a doctor who goes to Africa to help monkeys.

1960
Jane arrives in Gombe, Africa.

1961
Jane first sees chimps using tools.

Telling Her Story

Over the next 40 years, Jane wrote books about her exciting discoveries. She learned that chimpanzees live in close family groups and make friendships that last a lifetime. They hunt, and they teach their children. They can be happy or sad, angry or afraid.

And it all started with one woman who knew how to sit quietly—and watch carefully.

294

1970

1980

1990

1977
Jane founds the Jane Goodall Institute, which helps protect chimps and the forests.

1986
Jane begins to tell people around the world about the needs of chimps.

Think Critically

R2.3
R2.5
R2.6
R2.7
W1.1

1. In what year did Jane Goodall discover that chimpanzees use tools? GRAPHIC AIDS

2. Why did Jane Goodall not see the chimpanzees when she first arrived at Gombe? CAUSE/EFFECT

3. Why was Jane Goodall amazed when she saw David Greybeard using tools? IMPORTANT DETAILS

4. Why did the author tell about some of the chimps' names and behaviors? AUTHOR'S PURPOSE

5. **WRITE** What have other scientists learned about chimpanzees because of Jane Goodall? Use details and information from the selection. EXTENDED RESPONSE

CALIFORNIA STANDARDS
ENGLISH-LANGUAGE ARTS STANDARDS—Reading 2.3 Use knowledge of the author's purpose(s) to comprehend informational text; **Reading 2.5** Restate facts and details in the text to clarify and organize ideas; **Reading 2.6** Recognize cause-and-effect relationships in a text; **Reading 2.7** Interpret information from diagrams, charts, and graphs; **Writing 1.1** Group related ideas and maintain a consistent focus.

Meet the Author
Charnan Simon

Charnan Simon loves books. When she was a young girl, she visited the library at least once a week.

Charnan Simon has written dozens of books and articles for children. Her favorite things to do are reading, writing, and spending time with her family.

GO online www.harcourtschool.com/reading

297

Chimp Computer Whiz

from *Ask*

Keo never forgets a face.

Keo is a chimpanzee who lives at Lincoln Park Zoo in Chicago. Five times a week, he sits in front of a special computer screen. The screen flashes the face of a chimp he's never met. When Keo touches the picture of the chimp, he gets treats. Next, the screen flashes two pictures. One is of the first chimp, and one is of a new chimp. If Keo touches the picture of the first chimp, he gets another treat.

Keo plays this game 30 times each day. After months of practice, he can now run through all 30 new faces in just a few minutes.

Two other apes at the zoo, a chimp and a gorilla, are using computers to learn the numbers 1 to 9.

Working on the computer is voluntary. So far, only three of the nine apes that have tried it have stayed with it.

Scientists hope that all the apes at the zoo will soon use computer programs to tell which foods they like best and which activities they prefer. Watching the apes use computers should help scientists learn more about how the animals think.

Connections

Comparing Texts

❶ How are the chimpanzees in "Watching in the Wild" and "Chimp Computer Whiz" alike?

❷ What animal would you like to observe? Tell why.

❸ What other methods can scientists use to learn about animals?

Phonics

R1.1

Make a Chart

Write the words *hair* and *care* in a chart. Below each word, write three more words that have the same spelling and sound as the underlined letters. Read your lists to a partner.

hair	care
fair	glare

Fluency Practice

R1.6

Read with a Partner

Read "Watching in the Wild" aloud with a partner. Take turns reading one page at a time. Work on reading each sentence at the speed in which you usually speak.

Writing

W1.1

Write About an Event

Write about important events in your life. Tell about them in the order in which they happened. Use a chart to plan what you will tell about first, next, and last.

My Writing Checklist

Writing Trait → Word Choice

✔ I use a chart to plan my writing in time order.

✔ I use words that help the reader picture what is happening.

✔ I use words like *first, next,* and *last.*

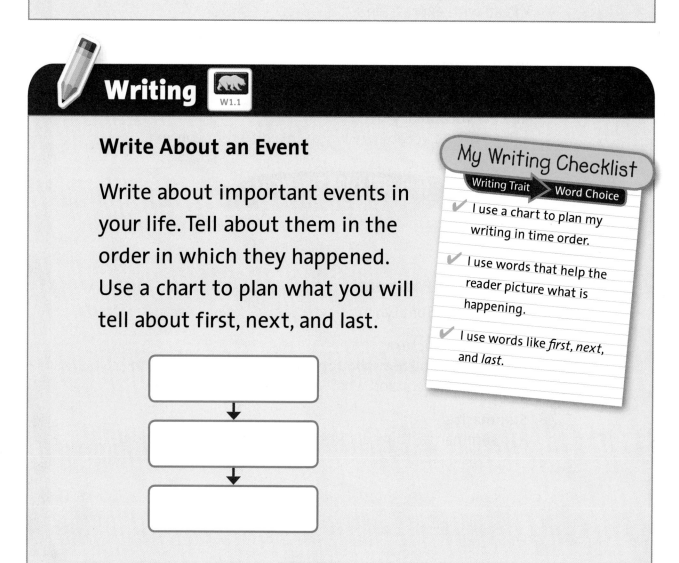

Reading 2.5 Restate facts and details in the text to clarify and organize ideas; **Writing 1.1** Group related ideas and maintain a consistent focus.

301

Contents

Interview

READERS' THEATER

Town Hall 304

Build Fluency
• Read with expression.
• Read at a rate that sounds like natural speech.

Build Vocabulary
• Read, write, and learn the meanings of new words.

Review Vocabulary
• Read theme vocabulary words in a different context.

COMPREHENSION STRATEGIES
Review

Fable

A Time for Patience 316
adapted by Tom Lynch

Use Story Structure
• Use what you know about how stories are arranged to help you understand what you read.

Summarize
• To summarize, think about the main ideas of a selection.

Readers' Theater
INTERVIEW

Town Hall

Reading Fiction
FABLE

A Time for Patience

SILVERTON CITY 1908 HALL

READERS' THEATER

report

feasible

accomplish

serve

area

attend

R1.6

Reading for Fluency

When you read a script aloud,

- think about how the characters feel to help you read with expression.

- read at the same speed as a speaker would say the lines.

CALIFORNIA STANDARDS
ENGLISH-LANGUAGE ARTS STANDARDS—
Reading 1.6 Read aloud fluently and accurately and with appropriate intonation and expression.

town hall

Town Hall

Roles

Teacher   Mayor

Kris   Town Leader 1

Robin   Town Leader 2

Setting

Town hall of a small town

Teacher: Good morning, Mayor. I'd like you to meet Kris and Robin, two of my students.

Kris: The students at our school have questions about the new park the town is building.

Robin: We'd like to ask you and some other town leaders our questions. Then we'll report back to our classmates.

Mayor: We'll be happy to answer your questions.

305

Kris: Why did you decide to build a park?

Mayor: The people in our town need a place to go with their families.

Robin: What kinds of things will be at the park?

Mayor: I'm happy to tell you that there will be a playground! In a town the size of ours, people have many interests. Different people in our town want different things.

Town Leader 1: We asked people to tell us what things they wanted in the new park.

306

Town Leader 2: People sent many letters to Town Hall, and we read all of them.

Kris: So, are you building everything that the citizens asked for?

Mayor: No, that wouldn't be feasible.

Robin: How did you decide what to build?

Mayor: We looked carefully at everything that people asked for. We were very serious about building what people wanted, but we had to make choices.

307

Fluency Tip

Robin is curious. How should you read her line?

Town Leader 1: Coming up with a good plan for the park was very difficult to accomplish.

Town Leader 2: It was hard work, but it was worth it.

Kris: Why do you say that?

Town Leader 2: By listening to everyone, we were better able to serve the community.

Robin: What do you mean by serving the community?

Mayor: A town's leaders are supposed to help *all* of the people who live there. We need to make sure that we take care of everyone.

308

playground

Teacher: You just reminded me of what we're studying in school.

Kris: Me, too. We've been learning about what town leaders do.

Robin: Before we talked with you, I never thought that running a town could be so much work.

Mayor: Parts of it are really pretty simple. Most people in town agreed that we needed a new playground in the park. Deciding to build one was easy.

Town Leader 1: Lots of people also wanted bike paths.

Town Leader 2: So we decided to have lots of bike paths in the park. Then the bikes wouldn't crowd the people who walk and jog.

309

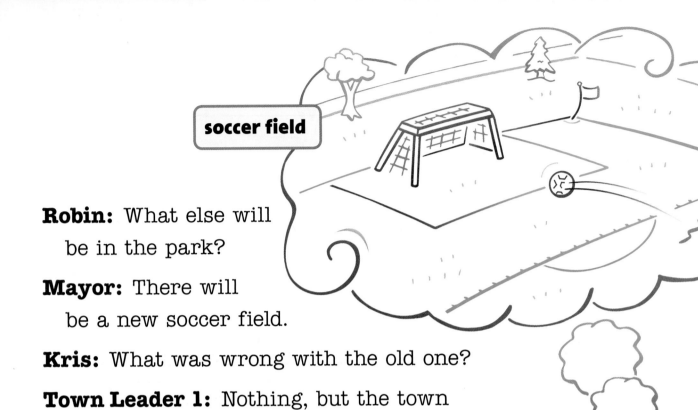

soccer field

Robin: What else will be in the park?

Mayor: There will be a new soccer field.

Kris: What was wrong with the old one?

Town Leader 1: Nothing, but the town needed more than one.

Town Leader 2: So many children in our town play soccer that we needed a second field.

Robin: I can see that you are building lots of things for children, but what about for grown-ups?

Mayor: We're making a big picnic area for families who come to the park on weekends and holidays. We're also adding lots of park benches so people can sit and be comfortable.

picnic area

Fluency Tip

The mayor is explaining something. Say these lines at a speed that others will be able to understand.

Town Leader 1: We also decided to make an area where people could let their dogs run.

Town Leader 2: There are a lot of dog owners in our town. They told us that their dogs needed a place to play. The problem was that other people didn't like the idea of dogs running around.

Mayor: We thought about it and figured out a way to make everyone happy. Now we will have a special place where dogs can run and not bother other people.

bandstand

Kris: It sounds as if you put in something for everyone. Is there anything else you want to tell us about?

Mayor: Yes, there is. We will also have a place where we can have music shows.

Robin: What gave you that idea?

Town Leader 1: We knew that some other towns had music shows in the summer.

312

Town Leader 2: It seemed like a good idea to do it here, too.

Kris: Did people ask for it?

Mayor: No, they didn't, but we thought it was a good idea anyway.

Town Leader 1: When we started telling people about it, they all got excited.

Town Leader 2: We will have music shows and plays that people of all ages will want to attend.

313

Teacher: Thanks for answering all of our questions. I don't think that we have any more.

Robin: I do have one more question. When will the new park open?

Town Leader 1: Our plan is to open it on the Fourth of July.

Town Leader 2: We're going to have a big party.

314

Mayor: The whole town will be invited. We're going to have music and lots of games.

Kris: I know where I'm going for the Fourth of July!

Robin: Me, too. I can't wait!

Fluency Tip

An exclamation point shows strong feeling. Read this line with feeling.

315

COMPREHENSION STRATEGIES
Review

Reading a Fable

Bridge to Reading Fiction Fables are stories that have been told for a long time. These stories are used to teach lessons about life. The notes on page 317 show some of the features of a fable. Look for these features each time you read a fable.

Review the Focus Strategies

R2.5

You can also use the strategies you learned in this theme to help you read fables.

Use Story Structure
Use what you know about how stories are arranged to help you understand what you read. Think about the fable's characters, setting, problem, and solution.

Summarize
Tell about the most important ideas in one or two sentences.

Use comprehension strategies as you read "A Time for Patience" on pages 318–319.

CALIFORNIA STANDARDS
ENGLISH-LANGUAGE ARTS STANDARDS—Reading 2.5 Restate facts and details in the text to clarify and organize ideas.

TITLE
The title gives you clues to what the fable will be about.

A TIME FOR PATIENCE

adapted and illustrated by
Tom Lynch

Sniffing for food one day, a hungry Fox came upon a shepherd's lunch sack hidden in a hollow old tree. So he squeezed into the tree. He gobbled up all the bread and meat that he found. His belly became so full that the Fox could not fit through the hole in the tree again. As much as he tried, he could not get out.

Hearing him cry out, another Fox came running to help.

"Why don't you stay in there for a while?" said the other Fox. "Wait until you get as thin as you were when you first went in. Then you will be able to slip out easily!"

**So remember!
Time and patience can solve
many problems.**

PROBLEM AND SOLUTION
The plot of a fable has a clear problem and solution.

MORAL
The moral of the fable is the lesson. The moral is usually found at the end of the fable.

Apply the Strategies Read the fable "A Time for Patience." As you read, stop and think about how you are using comprehension strategies.

Stop and Think

How can you use story structure to help you understand?
What parts of the fable would you use to summarize it?

A TIME FOR PATIENCE

adapted and illustrated by
Tom Lynch

Sniffing for food one day, a hungry Fox came upon a shepherd's lunch sack hidden in a hollow old tree. So he squeezed into the tree. He gobbled up all the bread and meat that he found. His belly became so full that the Fox could not fit through the hole in the tree again. As much as he tried, he could not get out.

Hearing him cry out, another Fox came running to help.

"Why don't you stay in there for a while?" said the other Fox. "Wait until you get as thin as you were when you first went in. Then you will be able to slip out easily!"

**So remember!
Time and patience can solve
many problems.**

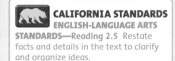

**CALIFORNIA STANDARDS
ENGLISH-LANGUAGE ARTS
STANDARDS**—Reading 2.5 Restate
facts and details in the text to clarify
and organize ideas.

READING-WRITING
CONNECTION

	Lesson 26 ❯	Lesson 27 ❯
Selection Titles	**Where on Earth Is My Bagel?** South Korea	**My Name Is Gabriela** Gabriela Mistral: A Poet's Life in Photos
Comprehension Strategies	Use Graphic Organizers	Use Graphic Organizers
Focus Skills	Cause and Effect	Cause and Effect

🐻 **CALIFORNIA STANDARDS**
ENGLISH-LANGUAGE ARTS STANDARDS

🐻 Reading 2.6 Recognize cause-and-effect relationships in a text.

🐻 Reading 2.6 Recognize cause-and-effect relationships in a text.

320

Theme 6 Seek and Find

▶ *The Trip That Never Was,* Cristina Rodriguez

Lesson 28 ▶

Let's Go Rock Collecting
Pebbles

Monitor Comprehension: Reread

Words with *al* and *ough*

Reading 1.1 Recognize and use knowledge of spelling patterns (e.g., diphthongs, special vowel spellings) when reading.

Lesson 29 ▶

The Lizard and the Sun
Be Sun Safe

Monitor Comprehension: Reread

Make Inferences

Reading 2.5 Restate facts and details in the text to clarify and organize ideas.

Lesson 30 Review

Cross-Country Vacation
Summer Safety

Review Skills and Strategies

Reading 1.1 Recognize and use knowledge of spelling patterns (e.g., diphthongs, special vowel spellings) when reading; Reading 2.5 Restate facts and details in the text to clarify and organize ideas; Reading 2.6 Recognize cause-and-effect relationships in a text.

Contents

Cause and Effect. 324

Learn to find causes and their effects in a story.

Vocabulary. 326

Read, write, and learn the meanings of new words.

Where on Earth Is My Bagel?
by Frances Park and Ginger Park
illustrated by Grace Lin 328

• Learn the features of fiction.

• Use a graphic organizer to help you understand a selection.

South Korea by Susan E. Haberle. 354

Read about the country of South Korea.

Connections 356

• Compare texts.

• Review phonics skills.

• Reread for fluency.

• Write a paragraph.

Lesson 26

Fiction

Where on Earth Is My Bagel?

By Frances
Ginger

Illustrated b

Q & A

South Korea
A Question and Answer Book
by Susan E. Haberle

Nonfiction

323

Focus Skill

 Cause and Effect

A **cause** is the reason something happens. An **effect** is what happens because of the cause.

Read this sentence.

Tim was hungry all afternoon because he skipped lunch.

The first part of the sentence tells what happened because of something else. This is the effect.

The second part of the sentence tells why Tim is hungry. This is the cause.

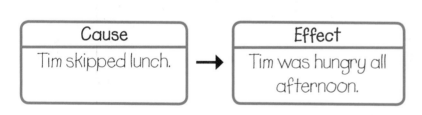

Cause		Effect
Tim skipped lunch.	→	Tim was hungry all afternoon.

Thinking about causes and effects can help you understand why story events happen and what makes characters act the way they do.

CALIFORNIA STANDARDS
ENGLISH-LANGUAGE ARTS STANDARDS—Reading 2.6 Recognize cause-and-effect relationships in a text.

Read the paragraph. Tell why Joy and Sam make a pizza.

Pizza Factory

Joy and Sam decided to make a pizza because they were hungry. Joy made the dough while Sam cooked the sauce. Joy added more flour because the dough was sticky. Sam added more spices because the sauce was too mild. Because of their hard work—and some extra cheese—Joy and Sam made a delicious pizza!

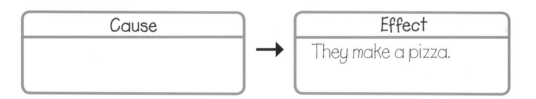

Cause		Effect
	→	They make a pizza.

 Try This!

Look back at the paragraph. Tell what causes Sam to add more spices.

 www.harcourtschool.com/reading

Vocabulary

smothered

pleaded

gently

grunted

replied

fragrant

Tess's Wish

Once upon a time, in a tiny village, there lived a girl named Tess. She dreamed of eating a slice of bread **smothered** with butter. The problem was that she had no oven to bake bread in. One night, Tess saw a star and made a wish.

"Oh, bright star," **pleaded** Tess. "Please send me an oven so that I can make a delicious loaf of bread."

326

For many days, Tess waited for an oven. Just as she was about to give up, a pig with a box knocked **gently** on her door.

"Did you make a wish on a star?" **grunted** the pig.

"Yes, I asked for an oven," **replied** Tess as she sniffed the box. There was something very **fragrant** inside.

"Well," said the pig, "the star was out of ovens, but it had plenty of bread with butter!

GO online www.harcourtschool.com/reading

Word Detective

 Where else can you find the Vocabulary Words? Look in your favorite magazine or in a book you are reading. Listen for the words on the radio. When you see or hear one of the words, write it in your vocabulary journal and tell where you found it.

Where on Earth Is My Bagel?

By Frances Park and Ginger Park

Illustrated by Grace Lin

Fiction

Genre Study

Fiction has characters, a setting, and a plot. Look for

- a problem and a solution.

- events that cause the characters to act the way they do.

| Cause | → | Effect |

Comprehension Strategy

Use graphic organizers like the one above to help you understand what is happening in a selection.

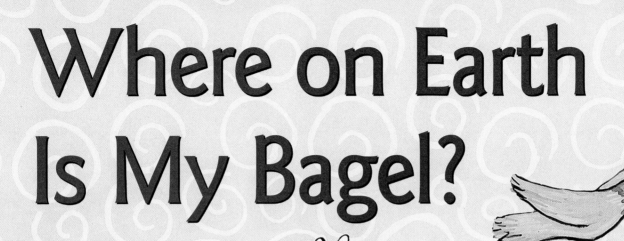

Where on Earth
Is My Bagel?

by Frances Park and
Ginger Park

illustrated by Grace Lin

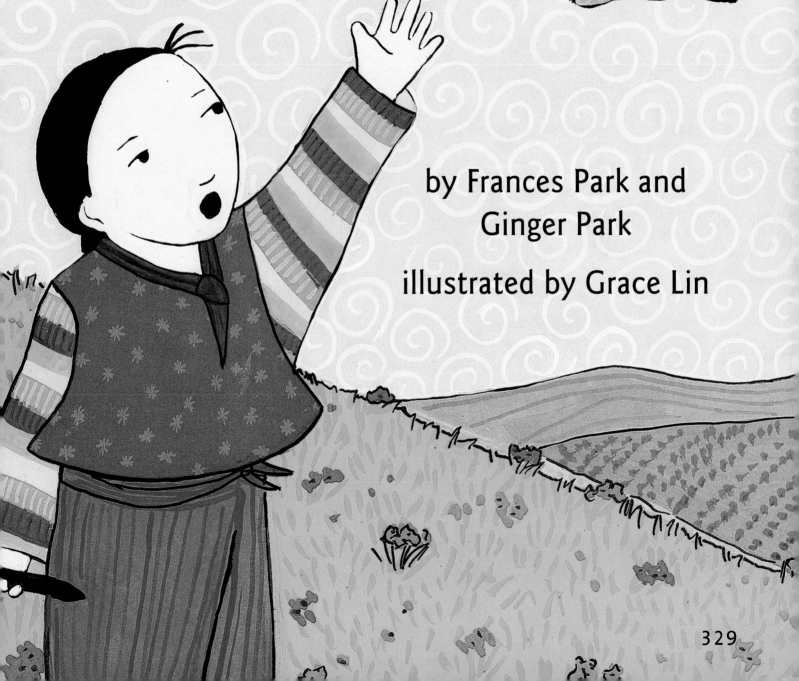

Once there was a boy named Yum Yung who lived in
a village where the mountains met the sky. There were
waterfalls rushing into streams of darting fish. There
were lilacs gently blossoming on every hillside.

But there were no New York bagels!

 How a New York bagel popped into Yum Yung's head was a mystery. Perhaps it came to him in a dream, smothered with cream cheese. Or maybe he heard sparrows singing of bagel crumbs in Central Park.

However it happened, Yum Yung could not stop thinking about a golden brown bagel with a curious hole in the middle. The very idea made his tummy growl and his mouth water.

Yum Yung declared:

"I want a bagel!"

Now dreaming about a New York bagel and actually eating a New York bagel were worlds apart.

Yum Yung wondered, "Where can I find a bagel?" He wondered and wondered, until he came up with an idea. "I will send a message!" he said.

So he sat on a rock and began to write:

Dear New York,
    I would like to order one bagel to go. Please send it to me as soon as possible.
            Respectfully yours,
            Yum Yung in Korea

Yum Yung carried his message to a mountaintop where birds flocked. Soon a pigeon landed on his shoulder. Yum Yung tied his message to the bird's tiny leg, and the pigeon flew off into the clouds.

"Pigeon," he cried out, "please return with my bagel!"

Yum Yung waited and waited on the
mountaintop. He waited until the sun dipped
below the mountain. He waited until the sky
was blanketed with stars. But the pigeon did not
return with his New York bagel.

Yum Yung decided that his bagel must be
lost. Perhaps the pigeon dropped his bagel on the
wrong mountaintop. Or maybe it was delivered
to the wrong person.

However it happened, Yum Yung would
not give up hope. A search was in order!
Yum Yung declared:
"Where on Earth is my bagel?"

335

The next morning Yum Yung visited Farmer Ahn, who was pushing his plow in a field of wheat.

"Excuse me, Farmer Ahn," Yum Yung said. "Have you seen my missing bagel?"

Farmer Ahn wiped the sweat off his forehead. "Bagel? What in a farmer's field is a bagel?"

"It is round and it has a hole in the middle," Yum Yung explained.

"Hmm," Farmer Ahn said with a nod. He pointed to his plow wheel. "Is that a bagel?"

Yum Yung frowned. "No, that is not my bagel."

"I am sorry, Yum Yung," Farmer Ahn said. "I know about wheat that grows from the rich brown earth, but I know nothing about bagels."

337

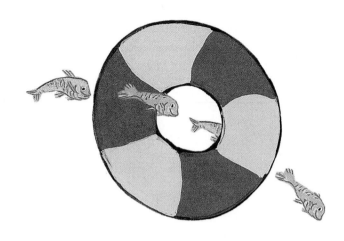

Next Yum Yung visited Fisherman Kee, who was on his boat shaking slippery fish out of his net.

"Excuse me, Fisherman Kee," Yum Yung shouted. "Have you seen my missing bagel?"

Fisherman Kee threw his net back into the water with a splash. "Bagel? What in the salty sea is a bagel?"

"It is round and it has a hole in the middle," Yum Yung explained.

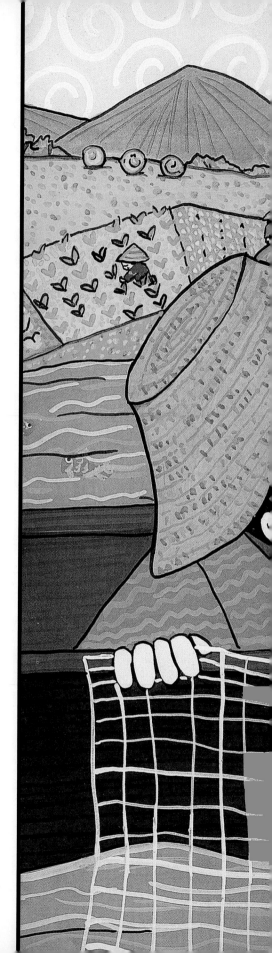

"Oh," Fisherman Kee said with a nod. He pointed to his life ring floating below. "Is that a bagel?"

Yum Yung frowned. "No, that is not my bagel."

"I am sorry, Yum Yung," Fisherman Kee said. "I know about fish that swim in the sea, but I know nothing about bagels."

339

Next Yum Yung visited Beekeeper Lee, who was collecting honey from a beehive.

"Excuse me, Beekeeper Lee," Yum Yung hollered from a distance. "Have you seen my missing bagel?"

Beekeeper Lee raised her bee veil. "Bagel? What in the sweet name of honey is a bagel?"

"It is round and it has a hole in the middle," Yum Yung explained.

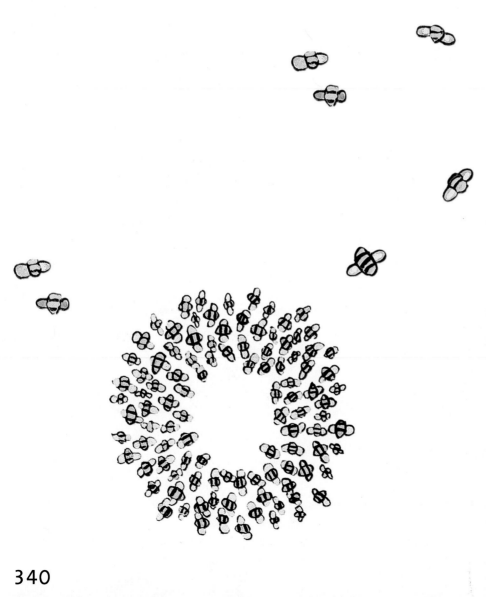

"Ah," Beekeeper Lee said with a nod. She pointed to the thick swarm of bees circling over her head. "Is that a bagel?"

Yum Yung frowned. "No, that is not my bagel."

"I am sorry, Yum Yung," Beekeeper Lee said. "I know about the buzzing business of bees, but I know nothing about bagels."

341

Yum Yung sat down on a quiet hillside and moaned. All hope for a bagel seemed lost!

Then a delicious smell tickled his nose. He sniffed curiously. Where was it coming from?

Yum Yung looked into the valley and blinked with delight.

There was Oh's Heavenly Bakery!

342

Yum Yung rushed into Oh's Heavenly Bakery, where Baker Oh was making one of her famous rice cakes.

"Baker Oh," Yum Yung pleaded, "please tell me you have my missing bagel!"

Baker Oh sprinkled a few pine nuts on the rice cake. "Bagel? What in a baker's kitchen is a bagel?"

"It is round, and it has a hole in the middle," Yum Yung explained.

"I am very sorry, Yum Yung," Baker Oh said. "I have not seen your missing bagel. But maybe that pigeon tapping at the window has better news for you."

Baker Oh opened the window. The bird flew in and landed on Yum Yung's shoulder—with a message!

While Baker Oh fed the pigeon rice cake crumbs, Yum Yung read the message aloud.

Dear Yum Yung,

Thanks a million for your order of one bagel to go. I'm real sorry, but my bagels only stay fresh on the same day they're made. So I'll do the next best thing and send you the secret recipe for my number one New York bagel!

P.S.
recipe on
other side

Good luck!

Joe
From Joe's To-Go Bagels

Baker Oh studied the recipe, then frowned.

"I am afraid I do not have all the special ingredients to make a New York bagel, Yum Yung. My sweet rice cakes are made with rice, sugar, and water. This bagel calls for flour, sea salt, and honey."

Yum Yung jumped. "Did you say flour, sea salt, and honey?"

"Yes," Baker Oh replied.

"I will return!" Yum Yung promised.

And indeed he did return—with Farmer Ahn and Fisherman Kee and Beekeeper Lee.

"I have the flour!" exclaimed Farmer Ahn.

"I have the sea salt!" exclaimed Fisherman Kee.

"And I have the honey!" exclaimed Beekeeper Lee.

It was time to make a New York bagel!

Baker Oh tied an apron around Yum Yung's waist. Following the recipe, Yum Yung instructed Farmer Ahn to sift flour into a mixing bowl. He instructed Fisherman Kee to sprinkle in the sea salt. He instructed Beekeeper Lee to spoon in the golden honey. Then Baker Oh poured in the water and tossed in a pinch of yeast.

Yum Yung kneaded the fragrant dough and formed it into a ring shape. He perfected the edges, especially for the hole in the middle. He dropped the dough into a large pot of simmering water. Minutes later, it floated to the top.

Then Yum Yung sprinkled it with sesame seeds, and into the oven it went.

Yum Yung watched the dough magically puff higher and higher until it nearly filled the whole oven—until it was a golden brown bagel.

The bagel was so big that Farmer Ahn, Fisherman Kee, Beekeeper Lee, and Baker Oh had to help Yum Yung carry it out of Oh's Heavenly Bakery. They all grunted as they set the bagel down under a persimmon tree on the quiet hillside. Yum Yung broke off a piece of the bagel for each of his friends.

"Hmm!" said Farmer Ahn.

"Oh!" said Fisherman Kee.

"Ah!" said Beekeeper Lee.

"Mmm!" said Baker Oh.

349

The moment had finally come for Yum Yung
to eat his New York bagel.

He closed his eyes and took his first bite. It
was a perfect bagel with a hint of honey so sweet
it made him sigh. It was soft and plump and chewy
and delicious all in one bite. It was so heavenly he
could even taste the curious hole in the middle!

Yum Yung declared:

"At last I have my bagel!"

Think Critically

R2.5
R2.6
R3.2
W1.1
W2.1b

1 Why does Yum Yung write a message to New York?

 CAUSE AND EFFECT

2 Why does Yum Yung visit the farmer, the fisherman, and the beekeeper? IMPORTANT DETAILS

3 Do you think Yum Yung could have made the bagel by himself? Why or why not? DRAW CONCLUSIONS

4 How might the ending be different if Yum Yung hadn't been able to get one of the ingredients? MAKE INFERENCES

5 **WRITE** How are the characters in "A Chair for My Mother?" like the characters in "Where on Earth Is My Bagel" SHORT RESPONSE

CALIFORNIA STANDARDS
ENGLISH-LANGUAGE ARTS STANDARDS—Reading 2.5 Restate facts and details in the text to clarify and organize ideas; **Reading 2.6** Recognize cause-and-effect relationships in a text; **Reading 3.2** Generate alternative endings to plots and identify the reason or reasons for, and the impact of, the alternatives; **Writing 1.1** Group related ideas and maintain a consistent focus; **Writing 2.1b** Describe the setting, characters, objects, and events in detail.

351

Meet the Authors
Frances Park and Ginger Park

Frances and Ginger Park are sisters whose parents were born in Korea. They like to write stories together. Frances likes to use her imagination to write about make-believe places, while Ginger likes to write stories about Korean culture. They both love eating chocolate—and bagels, too!

GO online www.harcourtschool.com/reading

352

Meet the Illustrator
Grace Lin

Grace Lin is the middle sister of three girls. Her dream was to be an ice skater, and she often drew pictures of herself skating. She soon realized that her art was better than her ice skating. She changed her dream to becoming an artist. She enjoys writing and illustrating books about Asian culture.

South Korea

In "Where on Earth Is My Bagel?" Yum Yung wants a bagel sent from New York City to South Korea. New York and South Korea are almost 7,000 miles apart. That would be a very long distance for a bird to travel with a bagel!

Where Is South Korea?

South Korea is a small country on the Korean Peninsula. The peninsula sticks out from northeastern China. It is about the size of the U.S. state of Utah. The peninsula is split into two parts. North Korea covers the northern part. South Korea makes up the southern half.

The Land of South Korea

Mountains cover much of South Korea. The T'aebaek Mountains stretch along the east coast. Halla San is the country's tallest peak. It is located on one of South Korea's many islands.

New York

CHINA

NORTH KOREA

T'aebaek Mountains

Sea of Japan (East Sea)

0 50 100 Miles
0 50 100 Kilometers

⊛ Seoul
Inchon

SOUTH KOREA

Yellow Sea

Taejon

Sobaek Mountains

Taegu

Kwangju

Pusan

North
West East
South

Korea Strait

JAPAN

Halla San

Connections

Comparing Texts

1 How can "South Korea" help you understand "Where on Earth Is My Bagel?"?

2 When have you worked with others to make something special? Tell about it.

3 What other foods might someone order from the United States?

Make a Chart

Write the words *look* and *could* in a chart. Below each word, write two more words that have the same spelling and sound as the underlined letters. Read your words to a partner.

look	could
book	would

CALIFORNIA STANDARDS
ENGLISH-LANGUAGE ARTS STANDARDS—Reading 1.1 Recognize and use knowledge of spelling patterns (e.g., diphthongs, special vowel spellings) when reading; **Reading 1.6** Read aloud fluently and accurately and with appropriate intonation and expression.

Fluency Practice

R1.6

Readers' Theater

With a small group, read "Where on Earth Is My Bagel?" as Readers' Theater. Remember to pause briefly at a comma. Pause longer at a period.

Writing

Write a Paragraph

Write a paragraph about something that happened to you. Tell why it happened. Use a cause-and-effect chart to plan your writing.

My Writing Checklist

Writing Trait ▶ Ideas

✔ I use a cause-and-effect chart to plan my writing.

✔ My paragraph tells something that happened to me.

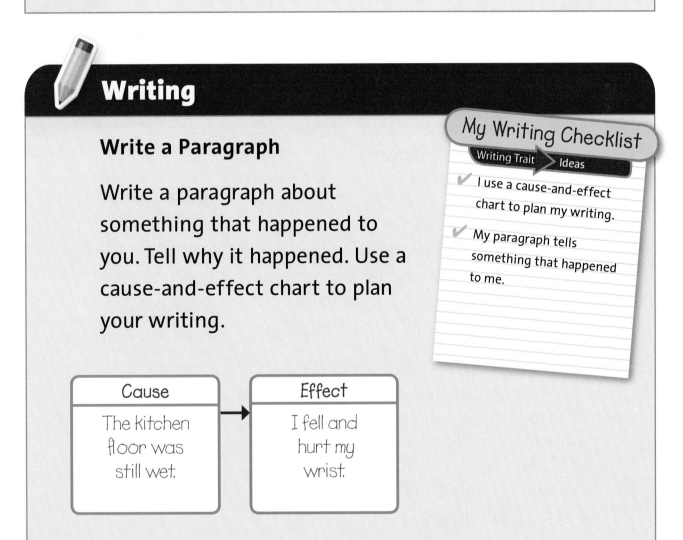

Cause	Effect
The kitchen floor was still wet.	I fell and hurt my wrist.

Reading-Writing Connection

Research Report

Before writing a **research report**, a writer gathers information from books and magazines and takes notes. I wrote this report after I read "Where on Earth Is My Bagel?"

Student Writing Model

<u>Carrier Pigeons</u>
by Leslie

Carrier pigeons are amazing birds. They can find their way home from more than 1,000 miles away. Because of this, they were used long ago to carry messages. They are still used this way for fun.

First, the birds are placed in cages and taken far from home. Next, a message is put into a tube, which is fastened to a pigeon's leg. Finally, the pigeon is set free to carry the message home.

How carrier pigeons find their way home is still a mystery. They may use the magnetic material in their beaks as a compass. Nobody knows for sure.

Writing Trait

CONVENTIONS Book and report titles are underlined.

Writing Trait

IDEAS Keep ideas in focus. Detail sentences should support the main idea.

Here's how I write a research report.

1. **I think about a topic I want to learn more about. Sometimes I find this topic when I read a book. I may have questions I want answered.**

> How far can carrier pigeons fly?
> How do they find their way home?

2. **I visit a library. I find information on my topic in books, in magazines, and on websites. I take notes on note cards.**

> How far can carrier pigeons fly?
> —more than 1,000 miles

3. I put my information in order. I use the cards to write an outline. An outline shows the order of main ideas and details.

> Outline
> 1. What are some facts about carrier pigeons?
>   a. find way home from more than 1,000 miles away
>   b. used long ago to carry messages
> 2. How do pigeons carry messages?
>   a. pigeon taken far away
>   b. message put in tube on leg
>   c. pigeon is set free
> 3. How do pigeons find their way home?
>   a. maybe by using magnetic material in their beaks
>   b. no one knows for sure

4. I write a draft of my report. I look over my report and make changes. I add a title.

Here is a checklist I use when I write a report. You can use it when you write a report, too.

Checklist for Writing a Report

- ☐ My report has an underlined title that tells what it is about.

- ☐ Each paragraph is indented.

- ☐ Each paragraph tells one main idea.

- ☐ Each paragraph gives details that support the main idea.

- ☐ I begin my report in an interesting way.

- ☐ My report follows an order that makes sense.

Contents

Cause and Effect 364

Learn to find causes and their effects in a selection.

Vocabulary 366

Read, write, and learn the meanings of new words.

My Name Is Gabriela by Monica Brown
illustrated by John Parra 368

• Learn the features of a biography.

• Use a graphic organizer to help you understand a selection.

Gabriela Mistral: A Poet's Life in Photos
by Alma Flor Ada and F. Isabel Campoy 386

Read a photo essay about Gabriela Mistral's life.

Connections 390

• Compare texts.

• Review phonics skills.

• Reread for fluency.

• Write a paragraph.

Biography

My Name is ✶ Me llamo
Gabriela

The Life of ✶ la vida de
Gabriela Mistral

by Monica Brown
Illustrated by John Parra

Gabriela Mistral

by Alma Flor Ada and F. Isabel Campoy

Photo Essay

Cause and Effect

R2.6

An **effect** is something that happens because of something else. The **cause** is what makes it happen.

As you read, think about what is happening in a story and why these things are happening. Look for words such as *because*, *so*, and *since*. They can help you find causes and effects.

Read this sentence. What is the cause? What is the effect?

Tomás loved his dog Buster, so he wrote a poem about him.

Cause		Effect
Tomás loved his dog, Buster.	→	Tomás wrote a poem about Buster.

Read the paragraph. Tell why Ryan likes Mrs. Flores's poems.

School Poems

Ryan's teacher, Mrs. Flores, writes poems. Every Friday, she writes a poem about something that happened in class during the week. Ryan likes Mrs. Flores's poems because they are funny. Mrs. Flores asks the class to write poems, too. She does this because she wants her students to learn to write well. Since Ryan is such a good writer, Mrs. Flores asks him to enter the school poetry contest.

Cause		Effect
	→	Ryan likes Mrs. Flores's poems.

GO online   www.harcourtschool.com/reading

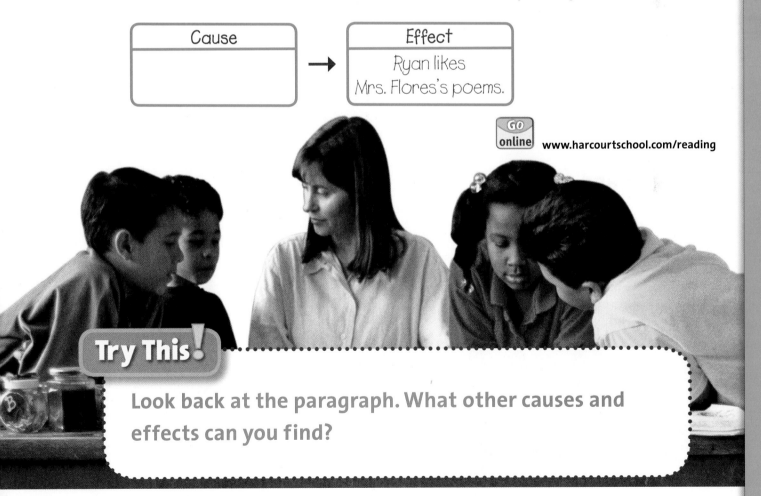

Try This!

Look back at the paragraph. What other causes and effects can you find?

Vocabulary

beyond

create

noticed

literature

award

grand

Wonderful Chile

Do you ever think about places that are **beyond** your neighborhood? One game that I play with my parents is called "Pick a Place." We each name a country we would like to visit and **create** a travel plan. Most often, I pick Chile.

One day, my mom said, "I've **noticed** that you're interested in Chile. Tell us more." Chile is my favorite country because my teacher has taught us a lot about it.

Sometimes my teacher shows us travel books about Chile. Other times she reads us works of **literature** by authors from Chile. One story won an important **award**.

Once some classmates and I pretended to go to Chile. We had a **grand** time climbing the Andes Mountains!

 www.harcourtschool.com/reading

Word Champion

Your challenge this week is to use the Vocabulary Words when you speak to family members and friends. For example, ask a family member to describe an **award** he or she has won. Each day, write in your vocabulary journal the sentences you spoke.

My Name is ✿ Me llamo
Gabriela

The Life of ✿ la vida de
Gabriela Mistral
by Monica Brown

Biography

Genre Study

A **biography** is the story of a person's life. Look for

- events in time order.

- events that cause changes in a person's life.

Cause	→	Effect

Comprehension Strategy

Use graphic organizers like the one above to help you understand what is happening in a selection.

My Name Is
Gabriela
The Life of Gabriela Mistral

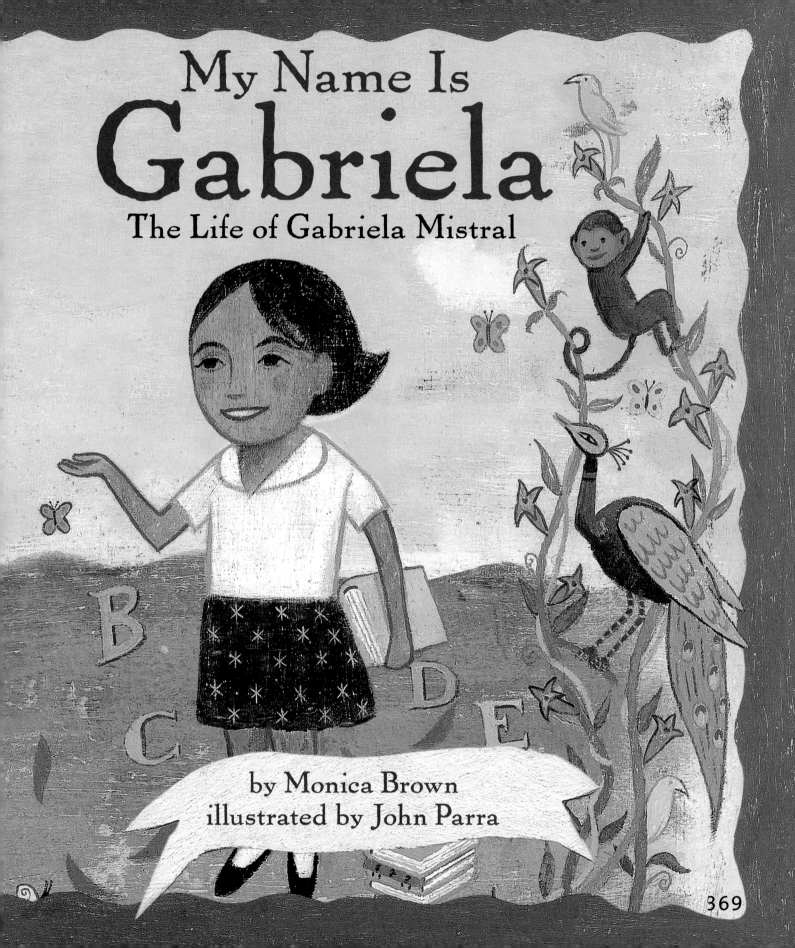

by Monica Brown
illustrated by John Parra

My name is Gabriela Mistral.
It is a name I chose myself
because I like the sound of it.

I love words and sounds and
stories.

When I was a little girl, I lived with my mother and Emelina, my sister, in a small house in the beautiful Elqui Valley in Chile. From my bedroom window I could see the Andes Mountains.

When I couldn't sleep, I would look up at the mountains and wonder what could be beyond them. Zebras with polka dots? Rainbow-colored flowers?

371

I loved words—I liked the sounds they made rolling off my tongue, and I liked the way they could express how I felt. When I saw a butterfly fluttering, I noticed the way the words *fluttering butterfly* sounded together—like a poem.

I taught myself to read so that I could read other people's words and stories. I read stories about princes and princesses and about birds and flowers.

I also liked to write poems, sing songs,
and tell stories, using the words that I knew.
I told stories about happy times and sad times,
about mothers and babies and little children.

I liked to play school with the children
of my village. I pretended to be the teacher,
and my friends, Sofia, Ana, and Pedro,
were my pupils.

Pedro would always say that I was mean because I made him write his ABCs until he knew all the letters of the alphabet. But I told him that the alphabet is important. How else would he **create** words and tell his stories without it?

In our pretend class we sang songs like

The baby chicks are saying
Peep, peep, peep.
It means they're cold and hungry.
It means they need some sleep.

That was Sofia's favorite song. During
recess we had fun, running and chasing
and laughing and playing.

When I grew up I became a real teacher and writer. I taught the children of Chile, and many of my students became teachers themselves.

I still wrote poems—happy poems, sad poems, stories of mothers and children. But I also wrote poems about animals—about parrots and peacocks and even rats!

378

I also traveled to far away places.
I never saw zebras with polka dots or
rainbow-colored flowers, but I met
wonderful children and their teachers.

I traveled to Europe—to France
and Italy.

I traveled to Mexico.

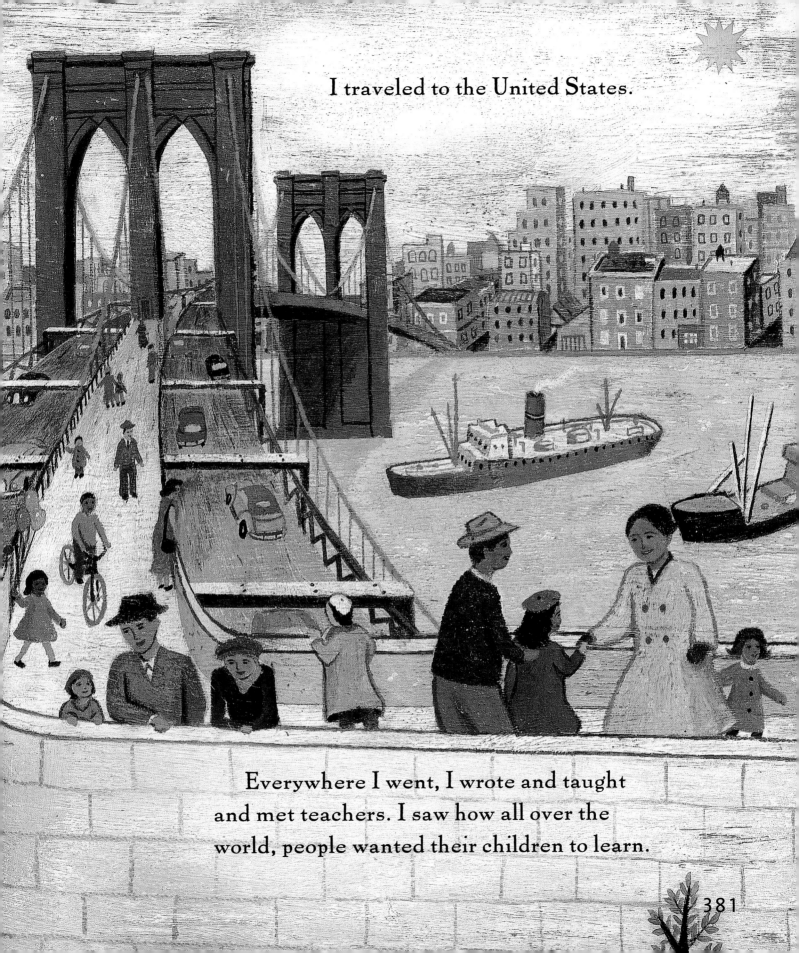

I traveled to the United States.

Everywhere I went, I wrote and taught
and met teachers. I saw how all over the
world, people wanted their children to learn.

My stories traveled the world with me.
People liked to read my happy stories, my sad
stories, my stories of women and children, my
stories of parrots and peacocks, of old lions
and of the fisherfolk, who slept in the sand
and dreamt of the sea.

And because people from all over the world
loved my stories so, I was given a very special
prize—the Nobel Prize for Literature.

When I accepted the grand award, I
thought of the beautiful mountains outside
of my window in Chile, of my mother and
sister, of the children of my village, and of
all the stories that still need to be told.

Think Critically

R2.3
R2.5
R2.6
W1.1

1 Why did Gabriela Mistral choose her name?
CAUSE AND EFFECT

2 Why did Gabriela want Pedro to learn his ABCs? IMPORTANT DETAILS

3 How do you think people around the world learn about Gabriela's poems and stories?
DRAW CONCLUSIONS

4 Why do you think the author wrote this biography? AUTHOR'S PURPOSE

5 **WRITE** What things does Gabriela Mistral do as a child that show she might become a teacher? Use examples from the selection.
SHORT RESPONSE

CALIFORNIA STANDARDS
ENGLISH-LANGUAGE ARTS STANDARDS—Reading 2.3 Use knowledge of the author's purpose(s) to comprehend informational text; **Reading 2.5** Restate facts and details in the text to clarify and organize ideas; **Reading 2.6** Recognize cause-and-effect relationships in a text; **Writing 1.1** Group related ideas and maintain a consistent focus.

Meet the Author and the Illustrator

Monica Brown

Monica Brown's life seems very much like Gabriela Mistral's. She has family in South America, and she is a writer and a teacher.

John Parra

John Parra grew up in a home filled with Mexican art. Today he enjoys creating pictures about Hispanic culture.

GO online www.harcourtschool.com/reading

385

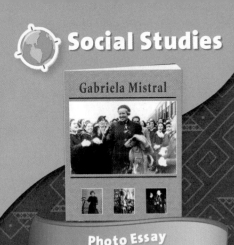

Photo Essay

Gabriela Mistral
A Poet's Life in Photos

by Alma Flor Ada and F. Isabel Campoy

From an early age, Gabriela loved to read. Her sister taught her songs and poetry.

They lived in Chile in a little house at the foot of the mountains. Gabriela liked to play outside. She loved the trees, the birds, and the plants around her house.

Gabriela Mistral became a teacher. She taught in schools in small towns in the mountains. She also taught in Santiago, the capital of Chile.

Gabriela Mistral was invited to Mexico to help make its schools and libraries better. While she was there, she wrote children's books. Her books used beautiful language to tell stories and legends from around the world.

Gabriela Mistral was proud of her heritage. Some of her ancestors were Spanish. Others were Native Americans who had lived in Chile for a long time. She felt that she was a part of two worlds.

Gabriela Mistral believed that all the countries of North America and South America should respect, protect, and help one another.

In a speech to the leaders of many nations, she presented her dream for peace between all countries. Her speech made people want to work for peace.

Gabriela Mistral went to Sweden to receive the Nobel Prize in Literature. She is the only Latin American woman writer who has received this prize.

Gabriela Mistral loved children. Many of her poems, such as this one, were written for and about them.

Rivers are children holding hands;
playing at running to the sea, tugging.
Waves are children holding hands,
playing at greeting the world, hugging,
and hugging.

Connections

Comparing Texts

1 How are "My Name Is Gabriela" and "Gabriela Mistral: A Poet's Life in Photos" alike? How are they different?

2 Gabriela Mistral pretended to be a teacher. What do you like to pretend to do?

3 How can you learn more about Gabriela Mistral?

Phonics R1.1

Make a Chart

Think of words in which the letters *aw* and *augh* stand for the vowel sound in *saw*. Write the words in a chart. Then create a rhyme with some of the words.

aw	augh
saw	taught
paw	caught

Read with a Partner

Read the selection aloud with a partner. Before you read each page, look for places where you can change your voice to be higher or lower. Look for words you want to stress.

Writing

Write a Paragraph

Write a paragraph about something you like to do. Tell why you like to do it. Use a cause-and-effect chart to plan your paragraph.

My Writing Checklist

Writing Trait ▸ Ideas

✔ I use a cause-and-effect chart to plan my writing.

✔ I use interesting details.

✔ I indent my paragraph.

Cause	Effect
I like the sound of rhyming words.	I like to write poems.

Contents

Words with *al* and *ough* 394

Learn to read words with *al* and *ough*.

Vocabulary 396

Read, write, and learn the meanings of new words.

Let's Go Rock Collecting by Roma Gans
illustrated by Holly Keller 398

• Learn the features of nonfiction.

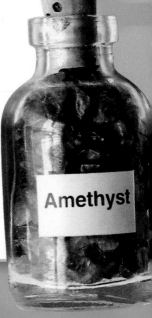

• Reread a section that you don't understand.

Pebbles by Valerie Worth
illustrated by Steve Jenkins 424

Read a poem about pebbles.

Connections 426

• Compare texts.

• Review phonics skills.

• Reread for fluency.

• Write a paragraph.

Amethyst

Lesson 28

Nonfiction

Let's Go Rock Collecting

Reading Rainbow Book

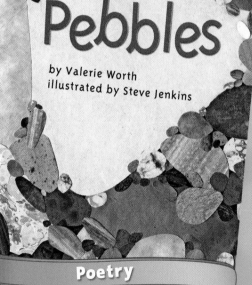

Mixed Gemstone

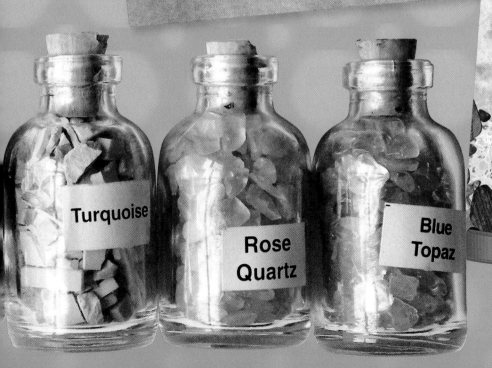

Turquoise

Rose Quartz

Blue Topaz

Pebbles

by Valerie Worth
illustrated by Steve Jenkins

Poetry

393

Phonics Skill

Words with *al* and *ough*

The letters **al** and **ough** can stand for the vowel sound in *salt* and *bought*. Read the words below. Do you hear the same vowel sound in each word?

chalk

thought

Now read these longer words.

sidewalk   **talkative**   **thoughtful**

Point to the letters in each word that stand for the vowel sound you hear in *salt* and *bought*.

CALIFORNIA STANDARDS
ENGLISH-LANGUAGE ARTS STANDARDS—Reading 1.1 Recognize and use knowledge of spelling patterns (e.g., diphthongs, special vowel spellings) when reading.

Read each word on the left. Tell which word on the right has the same sound.

	w<u>a</u><u>l</u>k	group cloud fought
	br<u>ought</u>	stalk tale made
	t<u>a</u><u>l</u>k	mask halt land

 www.harcourtschool.com/reading

Try This!

Read the word on the left. Which word on the right has the same sound?

b<u>ough</u>t

ham
chalk
please

Vocabulary

Build Robust Vocabulary

collection

common

rare

separated

settled

last

Stamp Collecting

Collecting stamps is fun and easy. To begin your **collection**, buy a packet of stamps. These stamps will be **common** ones, rather than **rare** ones, so they won't cost a lot of money. You can also cut stamps from envelopes.

Once you have some stamps, the first step is to sort them. For example, stamps can be **separated** by country or color. Then use scissors to trim the paper around the stamps. Never take a stamp off its paper by just pulling it. You might harm the stamp.

The next step is to soak the stamps. Put them into water that is at room temperature, and push them to the bottom until they have **settled** there. Soak them for about 15 minutes. Then peel them off the paper. Place the stamps flat on a paper towel, and press them with another towel.

The final step is to organize your stamps for display in your stamp album. If you care for your stamps this way, they will **last** for many years.

GO online www.harcourtschool.com/reading

Word Scribe

This week your task is to use the Vocabulary Words in your writing. For example, you might write about the steps you followed to organize a **collection** that you have. Each day, record in your vocabulary journal the sentences you wrote that had Vocabulary Words in them.

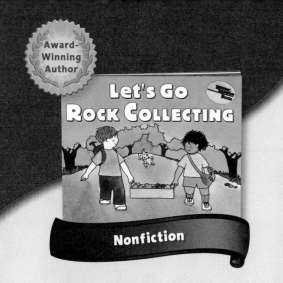

Let's Go
ROCK COLLECTING

Award-Winning Author

Nonfiction

Genre Study
Nonfiction gives facts about a topic. Look for

- paragraphs with main ideas and details.

- diagrams that give information.

K	W	L
What I Know	What I Want to Know	What I Learned

Comprehension Strategy
Monitor comprehension—Reread parts of a selection that are hard to understand or that have a lot of facts.

Let's Rock

Go Collecting

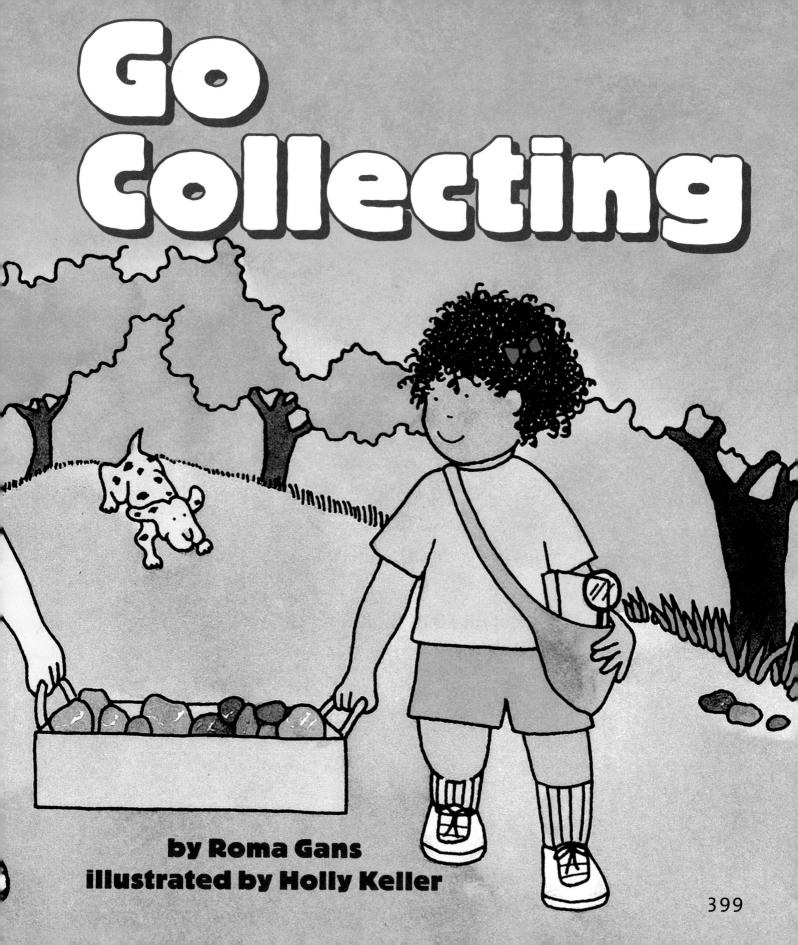

by Roma Gans
illustrated by Holly Keller

People collect all kinds of things. They collect coins, stamps, baseball cards, shells, toys, bottles, pictures, and cats. Some people collect things that are very old—the older the better.

The oldest things you can collect are rocks.
Most of them are millions and millions of years
old. Most kinds of rocks are easy to find. But
some, like diamonds and emeralds, are rare.
That's why they are valuable.

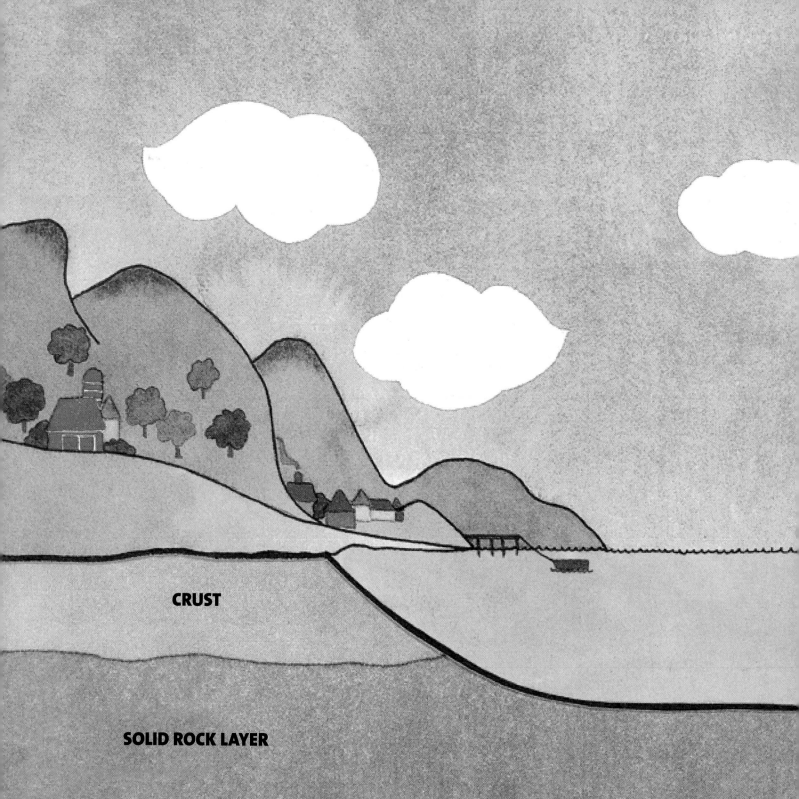

CRUST

SOLID ROCK LAYER

Rocks cover the whole earth. No matter where you live, you live on rock.

There is rock under city streets and country farms. And there is rock under every ocean, lake, and river.

CRUST

SOLID ROCK LAYER

The Romans built roads out of rocks. The roads are still used today. Things made with rocks last and last.

The rocks that make up the surface of the earth are called the earth's crust. Most of the crust is made of igneous rock. Igneous means made by heat.

Inside the earth it is very hot—hot enough to melt rock. The melted rock is called magma.

Sometimes the magma pushes through cracks in the crust. When magma comes to the surface, it is called lava. The lava cools and becomes very hard. It becomes igneous rock. Most of the earth's igneous rock comes from volcanoes on the seafloor.

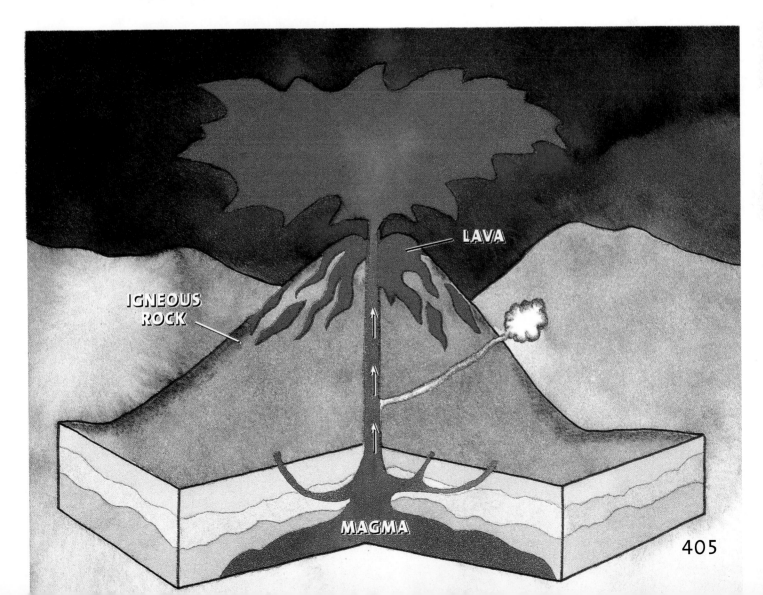

Granite is an igneous rock. It once was magma. Some granite is gray with small, shiny black and white crystals. Some granite has large pink, black, and white crystals.

GRANITE

The crystals in granite are called quartz. Some pieces of quartz are white like milk. Others are clear like glass.

QUARTZ

Sometimes quartz has bands of many colors. Jewelry is made from it. The marbles you play with may be made of banded quartz.

PURPLE QUARTZ

Basalt is another kind of igneous rock. It is usually dark in color—gray, green, or black. It is the most common of all igneous rocks.

BASALT

407

Mohs' Scale of Hardness

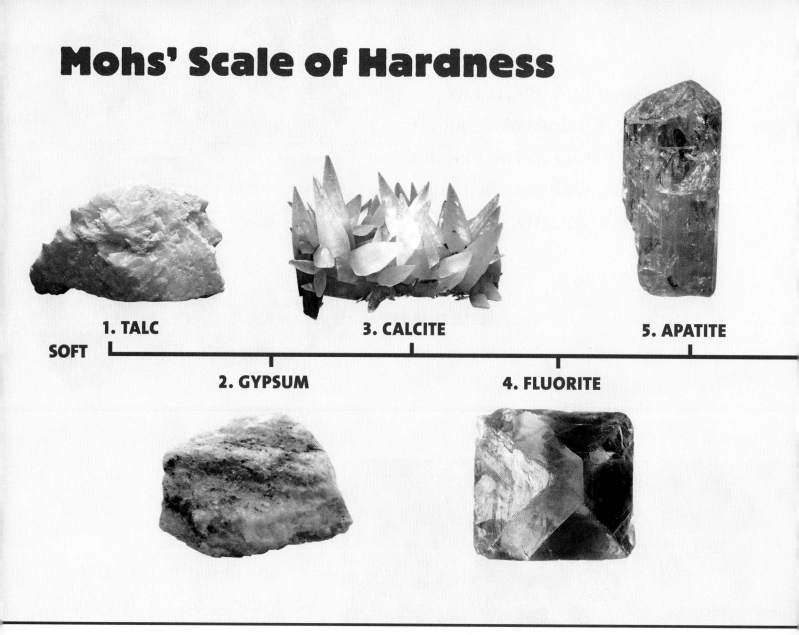

SOFT

1. TALC

2. GYPSUM

3. CALCITE

4. FLUORITE

5. APATITE

Not all rocks are hard. Some rocks are soft. Talc is so soft, you can pinch it into powder with your fingers.

Talc is number 1 on a scale for hardness of rocks. The scale is called "Mohs' scale of hardness," and it goes from 1 to 10. Quartz is number 7.

7. QUARTZ

9. CORUNDUM

HARD

6. ORTHOCLASE

8. TOPAZ

10. DIAMOND

Diamonds are number 10. They are the hardest rocks in the world. Each mineral on the scale can scratch the mineral below it. A fingernail has a hardness of about $2\frac{1}{2}$. So your fingernail can leave a scratch in talc, but not in calcite.

SAND, MUD, PEBBLES

SAND, MUD, PEBBLES

SAND, MUD, PEBBLES

SAND, MUD, PEBBLES

SEDIMENTARY ROCK FORMING

Not all rocks are igneous rocks. Some are made of sediments. Sandstone is one kind of sedimentary rock. It is made of grains of sand, mud, and pebbles.

Millions of years ago, sand was blown into rivers. The rivers carried the sand along and dropped it into lakes or oceans. Layer after layer settled on the bottoms of the lakes and seas. The top layers pressed down on the bottom layers. Slowly the lower layers of sand became stone.

You'll know sandstone when you see it. It is often soft and grainy. Rub it with your fingers, and grains of sand may come off.

Another sedimentary rock is limestone. It is
made of the shells of animals that lived millions
of years ago. Most often, limestone is white. But it
can be pink, tan, and other colors. Sometimes you
can see the outlines of shells in limestone.

Limestone is used to make cement. Cement
is then mixed with sand, gravel, and water
to make concrete for sidewalks.

Five thousand years ago the Egyptians built the pyramids out of limestone. They are still standing. Maybe someday you'll go to Egypt and see them.

Besides igneous and sedimentary rocks, there is a third kind of rock in the earth's crust. It is called metamorphic. Metamorphic means changed.

Slate is a metamorphic rock. Slate was once shale.

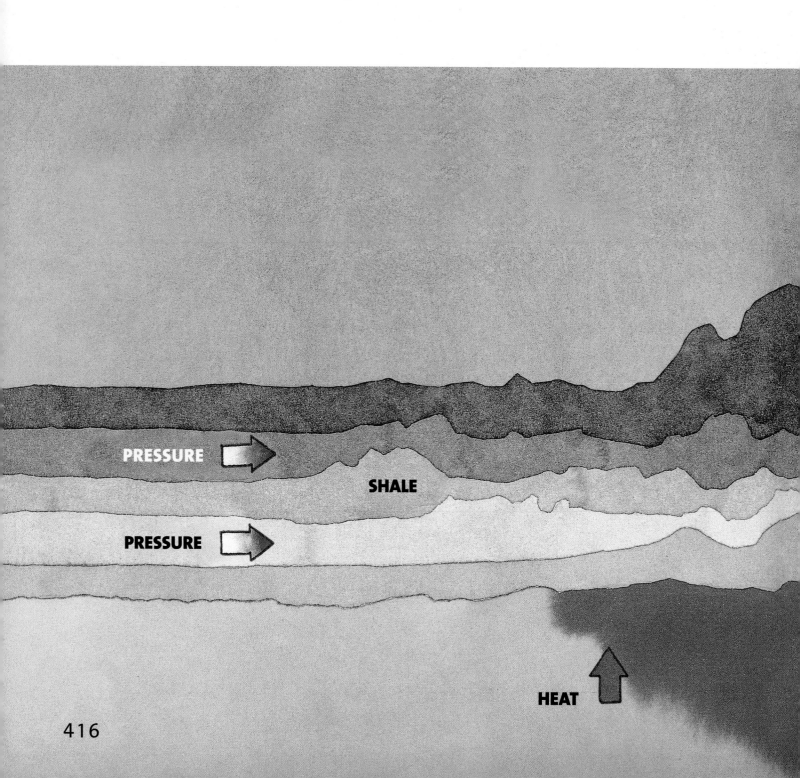

But over millions of years, tons and tons of rock pressed on it. The pressure made the shale very hot, and the heat and pressure changed it into slate. Most slate is gray, but some is black, red, or brown.

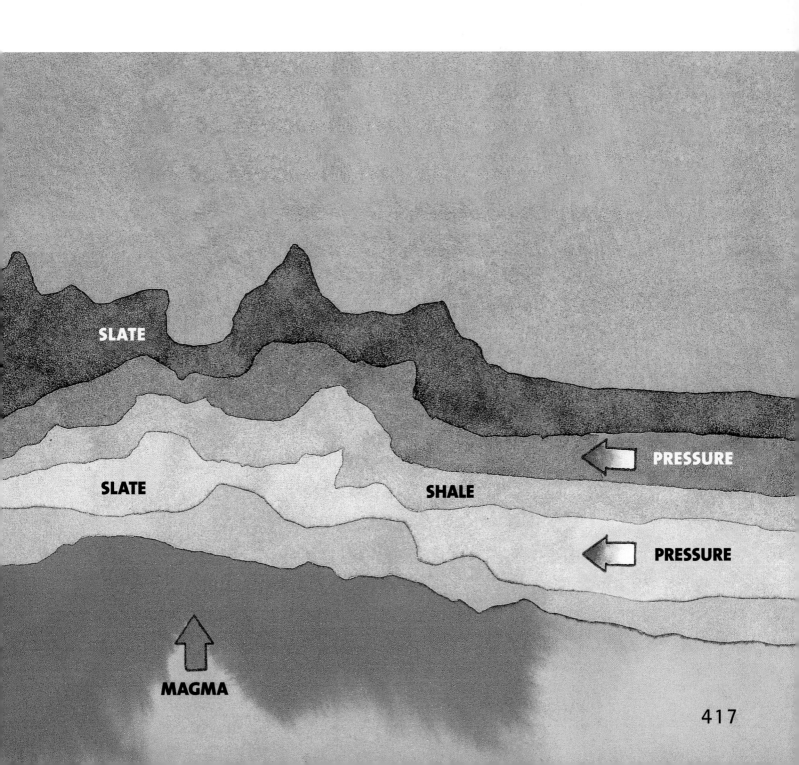

Other metamorphic rocks are made the same way slate is, by heat and pressure. Some metamorphic rocks are so changed, you can't tell what they once were.

GRANITE

Granite can turn into gneiss. It once was a piece of gray granite. Now it is darker gray, and its crystals have separated into layers.

GNEISS

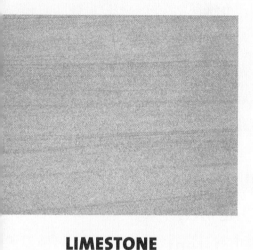

LIMESTONE

Limestone turns into marble. Some marble has colored marks that look like clouds.

MARBLE

SANDSTONE

Sandstone turns into quartzite. It may still look like sedimentary sandstone, but now it is much harder.

QUARTZITE

When you start collecting rocks, you'll find out how many different varieties there are. One way to start a collection is to look for rocks of different colors. You'll find there are pink rocks, black rocks, and pure white ones. There are gray rocks, and brown and yellow ones. See if you can tell what kind of rocks they are.

You can keep your small rocks in egg cartons.

You can keep larger ones in cardboard boxes with dividers like this one.

Rock collecting is fun. And one of the best things about it is that you can do it anywhere. Wherever you go, try to find new rocks and add them to your collection.

Think Critically

1 What is the meaning of the statement *No matter where you live, you live on rock?* MAKE INFERENCES

2 How is igneous rock different from sedimentary rock? COMPARE AND CONTRAST

3 In which kinds of rocks on Mohs' scale of hardness can your fingernail leave a scratch? USE GRAPHIC AIDS

4 How was limestone used long ago? How is it used today? IMPORTANT DETAILS

5 **WRITE** How is igneous rock made? Use the diagram on page 405 and information from the selection to explain. EXTENDED RESPONSE

CALIFORNIA STANDARDS
ENGLISH-LANGUAGE ARTS STANDARDS—Reading 2.5 Restate facts and details in the text to clarify and organize ideas; **Reading 2.7** Interpret information from diagrams, charts, and graphs; **Writing 1.1** Group related ideas and maintain a consistent focus.

Meet the Author and the Illustrator

Roma Gans

Roma Gans was one of ten lucky children. She felt lucky because her family believed reading was very important. She was taught that reading is an important way to learn about the world. This is the reason she started writing nonfiction books.

Holly Keller

When Holly Keller draws pictures for nonfiction books, she does a lot of research first. Then experts check the pictures to make sure they are correct.

 www.harcourtschool.com/reading

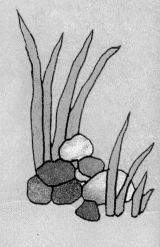

423

Pebbles

by Valerie Worth
illustrated by Steve Jenkins

Poetry

Pebbles

Pebbles belong to no one
Until you pick them up—
Then they are yours.

But which, of all the world's
Mountains of little broken stones,
Will you choose to keep?

The smooth black, the white,
The rough gray with sparks
Shining in its cracks?

Somewhere the best pebble must
Lie hidden, meant for you
If you can find it.

by Valerie Worth
illustrated by Steve Jenkins

Connections

Comparing Texts

1 How are "Let's Go Rock Collecting" and "Pebbles" alike? How are they different?

2 What do you like to collect? Why?

3 What are some ways people use rocks?

Phonics
R1.1

Make Sentences

Work with a partner to list words in which *al* and *ough* stand for the vowel sound in *walk*. Take turns choosing two words from the list and using both words in a sentence.

> I brought <u>chalk</u> for my teacher.

CALIFORNIA STANDARDS
ENGLISH-LANGUAGE ARTS STANDARDS—Reading 1.1 Recognize and use knowledge of spelling patterns (e.g., diphthongs, special vowel spellings) when reading; **Reading 1.6** Read aloud fluently and accurately and with appropriate intonation and expression.

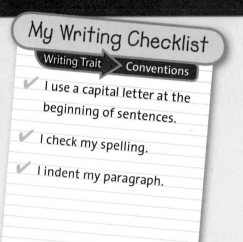

Fluency Practice

R1.6

Read with a Partner

Read "Let's Go Rock Collecting" aloud with a partner. Work on reading groups of words that go together. Help each other read each sentence correctly.

Writing

Write a Paragraph

Write a paragraph about a collection that belongs to you, a family member, or a friend. Include interesting details about the collection.

My mom collects shells whenever we go to the beach. She likes

My Writing Checklist

Writing Trait ▶ Conventions

✔ I use a capital letter at the beginning of sentences.

✔ I check my spelling.

✔ I indent my paragraph.

Contents

Make Inferences 430

Learn to make inferences while reading.

Vocabulary 432

Read, write, and learn the meanings of new words.

The Lizard and the Sun by Alma Flor Ada
Illustrated by Felipe Dávalos 434

• Learn the features of a folktale.

• Reread a page if you don't understand something.

Be Sun Safe from *US Kids* 464

Read about how to stay safe in the sun.

Connections 466

• Compare texts.

• Review phonics skills.

• Reread for fluency.

• Write a story.

Lesson 29

Folktale

A FOLKTALE IN ENGLISH AND SPANISH
CUENTO TRADICIONAL EN INGLÉS Y ESPAÑOL

THE LIZARD
and the SUN
LA LAGARTIJA
y el SOL

BY
Alma Flor Ada

Illustrated by / Ilustrado por
FELIPE DÁVALOS

BE SUN
SAFE

WAYS TO
STAY
SAFE
IN THE
SUN

Magazine Article

Focus Skill

 Make Inferences

Authors usually do not tell everything about the characters and events in a story. You often must **make inferences** to understand some parts of a story.

To make a good inference, use details from the story.

• Think about what has happened.

• Think about what the characters have said and done.

Then use what you know from real life. Think about events that have happened in your life that are like events in the story.

Details from the Story	+	What I Know from Real Life	=	Inferences

CALIFORNIA STANDARDS
ENGLISH-LANGUAGE ARTS STANDARDS—Reading 2.5 Restate facts and details in the text to clarify and organize ideas.

Read the paragraph. Tell about the story details and what you know from real life.

Dry Spell

The plants were drying up. So were the creeks that usually had a steady stream of water for the forest animals. Beaver sniffed the air. What was that smell? It held a hint of dampness. Then he checked the sky. What was that gathering above the far hill? It looked like a cloud with dark edges. Beaver watched the cloud. It was moving toward him.

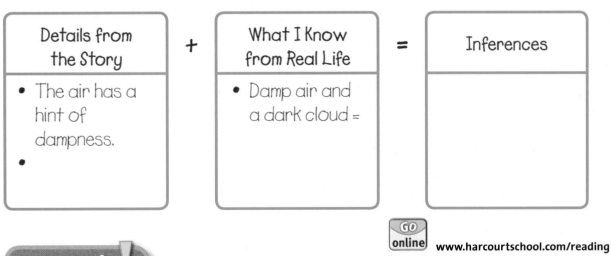

Details from the Story	+	What I Know from Real Life	=	Inferences
• The air has a hint of dampness. •		• Damp air and a dark cloud =		

GO online www.harcourtschool.com/reading

Try This!

Look back at the paragraph. What inferences can you make?

Build Robust Vocabulary

- entire
- peered
- majestic
- scampering
- budge
- discovery

Ledo the Great

My mom and I had looked through the **entire** pet store before I saw the pet I wanted. I **peered** into a glass tank and spied a blue and green lizard. A sign on the tank said, "Hi! I'm Ledo." This pet store also had fish and **majestic** birds. But I wanted Ledo as a pet. He was so cool!

I led my mom to Ledo's tank. The pet store manager was just starting to feed him fruit. Ledo was **scampering** around the tank.

432

I watched Ledo for a long time. He was fun to watch. He loomed over his water dish like a dinosaur over a lake.

Mom continued to look at the other animals, but I wouldn't **budge**. Nothing could make me leave Ledo's side. He was my great pet store **discovery**. Now Ledo the lizard has a new home with me.

 www.harcourtschool.com/reading

GO online www.harcourtschool.com/reading

Word Detective

Look for the Vocabulary Words outside of your classroom. You might look in a science book or visit a science website. In your vocabulary journal, write the words you see or hear. Tell where you found them.

Award Winner

THE LIZARD and the SUN
LA LAGARTIJA y el SOL
BY Alma Flor Ada
Illustrated by / Ilustrado por
FELIPE DÁVALOS

Folktale

Genre Study

A **folktale** is a story that has been told for a long time by a group of people. Look for

- a setting and characters from long ago.
- a lesson for readers.

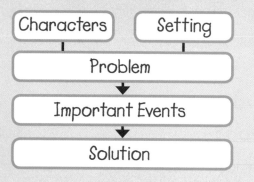

Characters | Setting
Problem
Important Events
Solution

Comprehension Strategy

Monitor comprehension— Reread a page if you do not understand something.

434

The Lizard and the Sun

by ALMA FLOR ADA

illustrated by FELIPE DÁVALOS

The whole world knows that the sun comes out every day. Some days, it shines brightly in a clear blue sky. Other days, clouds cover the sun and its light is much paler. When the clouds let loose their load of rain, the sun disappears behind a curtain of water.

There are places where it snows. During a snowstorm, the sun also stays hidden. But even when clouds, rain, or snow hide the sun, we know that it's still there. The story I am going to tell you happened a long long time ago, when the sun had really disappeared.

It had been many days since the sun had come out. Everything was dark. All of the plants, the animals, and the people were waiting anxiously for the sun to appear. But the sun did not come out, and everything remained in darkness.

The people were cold. The birds had stopped singing, and the children had stopped playing. Everyone was worried and afraid, for this had never happened before.

The animals decided to go out in search of the sun. The fish and the turtles looked in the rivers and lakes. But the sun was not there.

The green frogs and the wide-mouthed toads looked
through all the puddles. But the sun was not there.

The deer and the squirrels searched through the
forests. But the sun was not there.

The rabbits and the hares searched through the
fields. The jaguar searched through the green jungle,
where he lives. But the sun was nowhere to be found.

The birds searched through the branches where they had made their nests. And the majestic eagle flew over the mountaintops and the cones of the volcanoes. But no one could find the sun. And little by little, all of the animals stopped looking. All of them except for the lizard.

The lizard kept on looking for the sun. She climbed rocks, scurried up tree trunks, and peered under leaves, searching, always searching.

Finally, one day, she saw something very strange. She was scampering over some rocks when she saw that one of them was shining as though it had a light inside.

The lizard had seen many rocks in her life. She had seen rocks that were smooth and polished, and rocks that were rough and sharp. She had seen shiny gray rocks and dull dark ones. But she had never seen a rock that shone as much as this one did. It shone so brightly that it seemed to glow. So with great excitement, the lizard ran off to the city to share her discovery.

At last the lizard reached the city. Even though there had been no sunlight for many days, the people had kept on working. The barges floated softly on the waters of the lagoon, laden with fruits and flowers.

In the enormous marketplace, the vendors had laid out their wares on beautiful woven blankets. The pyramids of fruits and vegetables looked like tiny copies of the great stone pyramids that loomed over the city.

443

But without the sun's light, no one could see
the brilliant colors of the peppers and tomatoes,
the beautiful deep colors of the blankets and
shawls. Instead, the flickering torches that lit
the marketplace cast deep shadows.

And instead of the cheerful bustle of people buying and selling and having a good time, there was a low murmur of worried voices wondering how long this endless night might last.

445

The lizard did not stop to look at the barges or at the market's wares. She did not stop to look at the silent crowd that walked through the plaza. Instead, she headed straight for the grand palace and did not stop until she was in front of the throne.

Here, by the dim light of the torches, the lizard saw the great emperor. He wore sandals made of gold and a tall crown made of beautiful feathers.

"Sir, I have seen a rock which shone with a strange light," said the lizard.

"Move the rock, so you can see why it shines," ordered the emperor.

The lizard did what the emperor had commanded. She returned to where the rock lay and tried to move it. She tried to push it with her two front legs and then with her two hind legs. But the rock did not move. At last the lizard pushed the rock with her whole body. But the rock would not budge.

There was nothing left for the lizard
to do but go back to the city. She crossed
one of the wide bridges, passed by the
marketplace, arrived at the grand palace,
and went straight to see the emperor.

She found him sitting on the same
throne, surrounded by the smoke
of the torches.

"I'm very sorry, sir," she said. "I did everything I could, but I could not move the rock."

The emperor wanted very much to see this glowing rock, so he decided to go back with the lizard. But first he called for the woodpecker.

"I want you to come with us," the emperor said to the woodpecker.

And so the three of them, the emperor, the lizard, and the woodpecker, went to see the glowing rock.

450

When they reached the rock, the emperor said
to the woodpecker, "I want you to hit that rock
hard with your beak."

The woodpecker obeyed the emperor. He gave
the rock a sharp peck with his strong beak, and the
rock split open. And inside the rock was the sun,
all curled up and fast asleep.

The emperor was very happy to see the sun again.
The world had been very cold and dark without him.

"Wake him up, woodpecker," ordered the emperor.

And the woodpecker pecked several times on
the rock.

Tock, tock, tock, went the woodpecker's beak
as it struck the hard rock. The sun opened one eye,
but he immediately closed it again and went right
on sleeping.

"Wake up, Sun," said the lizard. "All of the animals have been looking for you."

But the sun did not answer. He just stretched a bit and went on sleeping.

"Wake up, Sun," said the woodpecker. "All of the birds have been waiting for you."

But the sun yawned an enormous yawn and kept on sleeping.

"Get up, Sun," said the emperor. "The entire city needs you."

But the sun just said, "Leave me in peace. I want to sleep."

The emperor knew that he had to do something. Without the sun, the plants could not grow, and his people would not have any food to eat. Without the sun, the children could not go out to play, the birds could not come out to sing, and the flowers would not bloom.

So the emperor said to the sun, "Wouldn't you like to see some beautiful dances? I will ask the finest musicians and dancers to play and dance for you. That will help you wake up."

"Well, if you want me to wake up, ask them to start playing their liveliest music, and to keep right on playing and dancing," answered the sun.

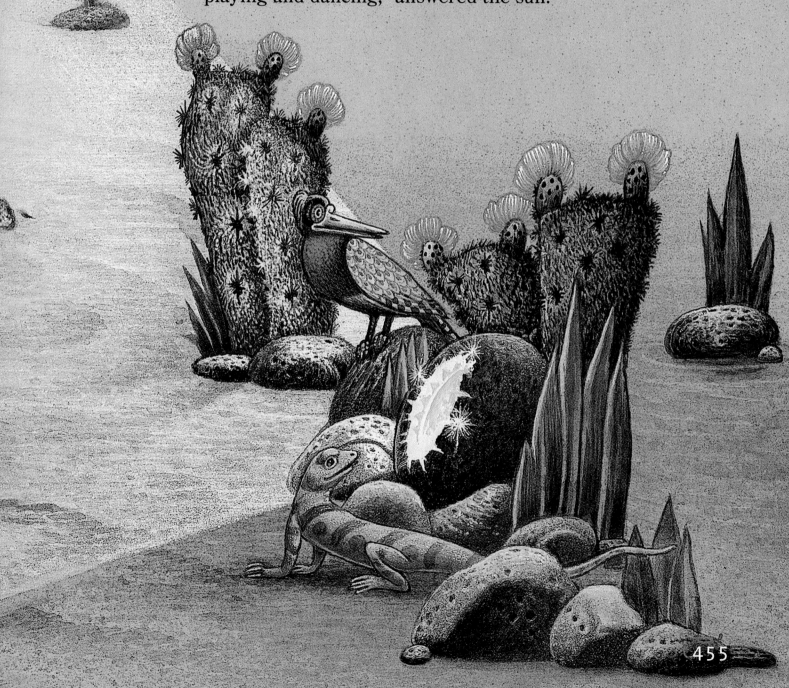

So the emperor called for the finest dancers
and musicians. The dancers, all adorned with
beautiful feathers of many colors, danced in the
plaza in front of the highest pyramid.

The loud, joyful music played on and on, and
the sun woke up, climbed to the highest point in
the sky, and shone down over everyone, lighting
the whole earth.

457

The emperor called for the emerald-colored lizard. He put her on the palm of his hand, and thanked her for having helped to find the sun. Then he called for the red-breasted woodpecker. He asked him to stand on his shoulder, and thanked him for having helped to wake up the sun.

Every year from then on, the emperor organized a great feast, with joyful music and beautiful dances, so that the sun would never again fall asleep, hidden away inside a rock.

And since that day, all lizards love to lie in the
sun. They like to remember the day when one of
their own found the sun's hiding place and helped
bring him back to give light and warmth to everyone.

Think Critically

R2.5
W1.1

1 Why do you think the sun is sleeping inside a rock? **Focus Skill** MAKE INFERENCES

2 Why is the lizard the one that finds the sun? DRAW CONCLUSIONS

3 Why do you think the emperor asks the woodpecker to break the rock instead of doing it himself? DRAW CONCLUSIONS

4 How does this folktale explain why lizards lie in the sun today? IMPORTANT DETAILS

5 **WRITE** Why is it important for the people and animals to find the sun? Use details from the story in your answer.

SHORT RESPONSE

CALIFORNIA STANDARDS
ENGLISH-LANGUAGE ARTS STANDARDS—Reading 2.5 Restate facts and details in the text to clarify and organize ideas; **Writing 1.1** Group related ideas and maintain a consistent focus.

MEET THE AUTHOR

Alma Flor Ada

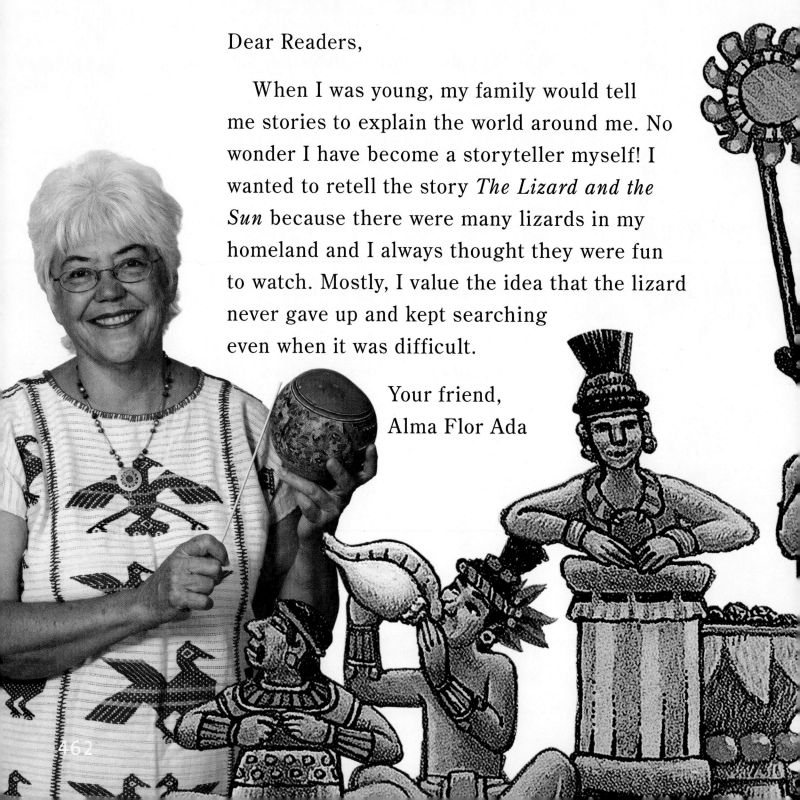

Dear Readers,

When I was young, my family would tell me stories to explain the world around me. No wonder I have become a storyteller myself! I wanted to retell the story *The Lizard and the Sun* because there were many lizards in my homeland and I always thought they were fun to watch. Mostly, I value the idea that the lizard never gave up and kept searching even when it was difficult.

Your friend,
Alma Flor Ada

MEET THE ILLUSTRATOR
Felipe Dávalos

Dear Reader,

I have always loved art and drawing. I enjoy painting and drawing pictures that are based on the art of my ancestors, the ancient Mexicans. I am also an archeologist. I try to put what I have learned about ancient cultures into my paintings.

Your friend,
Felipe Dávalos

GO online www.harcourtschool.com/reading

463

Magazine Article

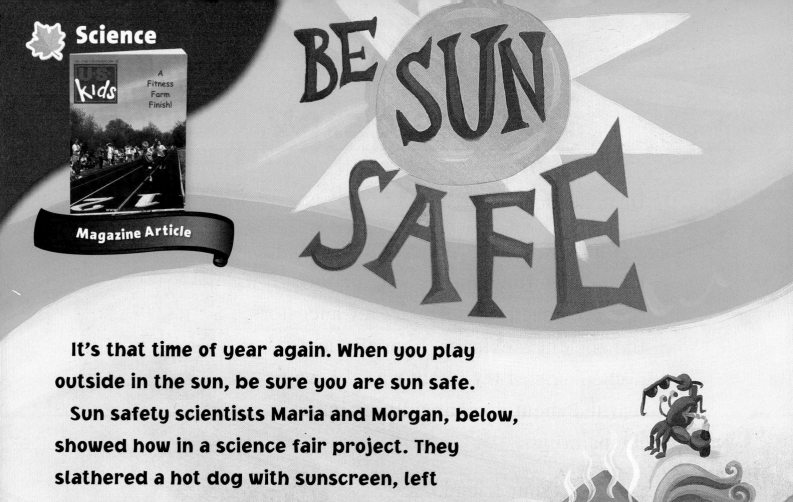

BE SUN SAFE

It's that time of year again. When you play outside in the sun, be sure you are sun safe.

Sun safety scientists Maria and Morgan, below, showed how in a science fair project. They slathered a hot dog with sunscreen, left another one bare, and put them under a heat lamp. The hot dog without sunblock didn't have a good day at all.

"It almost exploded," said Maria.

"But the dog with sunscreen didn't change at all," said Morgan.

The moral of the story? Always wear sunscreen outside, unless you want to end up as a real hot dog!

Connections

Comparing Texts

1 Compare "The Lizard and the Sun" and "Be Sun Safe." How are they alike and different?

2 How do you protect yourself when you are out in the sun?

3 How can you learn more about lizards?

Phonics

R1.1

Write Sentences

Work with a partner to list words in which *ea*, *eigh*, and *ey* stand for the long *a* sound. Write the words in a chart. Then write a sentence that uses one word from each column.

ea	eigh	ey
break	eight	obey
great	neighbor	they

They are great neighbors.

Fluency Practice

R1.6

Read with a Partner

Take turns reading "The Lizard and the Sun" aloud with a partner. Work on reading groups of words that go together. Help each other read each sentence correctly.

Writing

Write a Story

Write a story about another animal that likes the sun. Use a story map to help you. Tell how the animal gets the sun to shine more often.

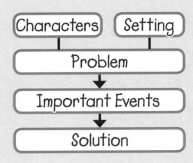

My Writing Checklist

Writing Trait ➤ Conventions

✔ I use a story map to plan my story.

✔ I put an end mark at the end of each sentence.

✔ I give my story a title.

Contents

READERS' THEATER

Travel Diary

Cross-Country Vacation 470

Build Fluency
• Use punctuation marks to help you read with expression.
• Group words together to make reading sound smoother.

Build Vocabulary
• Read, write, and learn the meanings of new words.

Review Vocabulary
• Read theme vocabulary words in a different context.

COMPREHENSION STRATEGIES
Review

Functional Text

Summer Safety 482
from *Weekly Reader*

 Use Graphic Organizers
• Review how to use a graphic organizer to help you organize information you read.

 Monitor Comprehension—Reread
• Remember to reread if you don't understand something.

Readers' Theater
TRAVEL DIARY

Cross-Country Vacation

Reading for Information
FUNCTIONAL TEXT

SUMMER SAFETY

469

delay

fantastic

spare

historical

impressive

upbeat

R1.6

Reading for Fluency

When you read a script aloud,

- read smoothly by grouping words that go together.

- use punctuation marks as clues to help you read correctly.

CALIFORNIA STANDARDS
ENGLISH-LANGUAGE ARTS STANDARDS—
Reading 1.6 Read aloud fluently and accurately and
with appropriate intonation and expression.

Cross-Country Vacation

ROLES

Dad	Terry	Mom
Cam	Nicky	Jessie

Scene One

PLACE
The family's house, in Columbus, Ohio

- - - - - - - - - - - - - - - - -

Dad: Okay, everyone, before you hop into the car, look at the camera and wave!

Terry: Good-bye, Ohio!

Mom: California, here we come! We're off without further delay.

Cam: We're driving to Aunt Fran's house for a visit. We'll be on the road for two weeks. This is the start of our video travel diary. Come along with us!

471

Nicky: Our vacation is going to be awesome. We'll be driving to some fantastic places!

Mom: We'll use the camera to record each place we visit.

Dad: By the end of the trip, we'll have a great video.

Cam: You'll feel as if you went with us!

Jessie: So, buckle your seat belts.

Nicky: Shut the doors. We have no time to spare.

Everyone: We're heading out to see new parts of the United States!

Scene Two

PLACE
The Abraham Lincoln Presidential Museum,
in Springfield, Illinois

Cam: Our first stop is an important historical site.

Terry: This is a cool place.

Jessie: We are in the hometown of our country's sixteenth President, Abraham Lincoln.

Cam: We're taking a tour of the Abraham Lincoln Presidential Museum. It has actual things from President Lincoln's life and times.

Tip

Group
in a way
you under.
what you ar
reading.

Abraham
Lincoln
Presidential
Museum

ABRAHAM LINCOLN PRESIDENTIAL MUSEUM

ROUTE

66

473

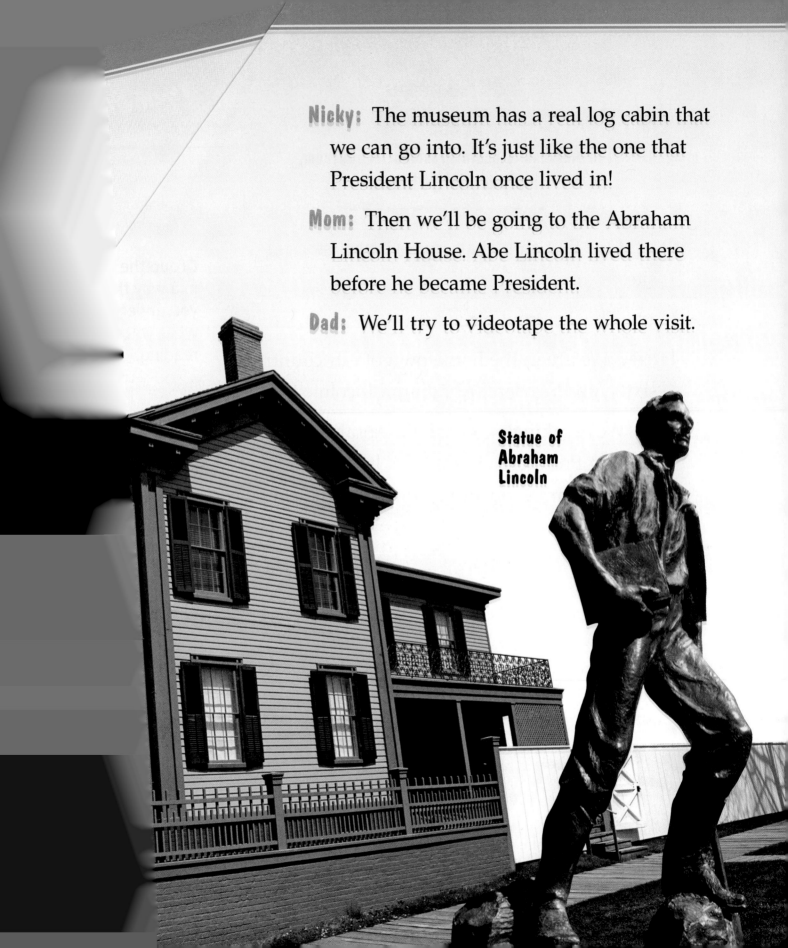

Nicky: The museum has a real log cabin that we can go into. It's just like the one that President Lincoln once lived in!

Mom: Then we'll be going to the Abraham Lincoln House. Abe Lincoln lived there before he became President.

Dad: We'll try to videotape the whole visit.

Statue of
Abraham
Lincoln

Scene Three

PLACE
Lake of the Ozarks State Park, Missouri

Jessie: Today we're walking through a field of wildflowers. We're heading down to the lake to go swimming and take a boat ride. I'm going to water-ski!

Terry: The flowers are so colorful.

Cam: They smell sweet, too, almost like honey.

Fluency Tip

Pay attention to commas as you read. Take a short pause at each comma.

475

Terry: Look, a butterfly! Do you think I can catch it?

Mom: Butterflies are fragile. Please don't touch them. Even if you touch them gently, you can harm them.

All the Children: Don't worry, we won't touch them!

Dad: We've been camping near the Lake of the Ozarks in a state park in Missouri. It's great to be out in nature.

Nicky: Animals depend on nature to live. That's why it's important to protect it.

476

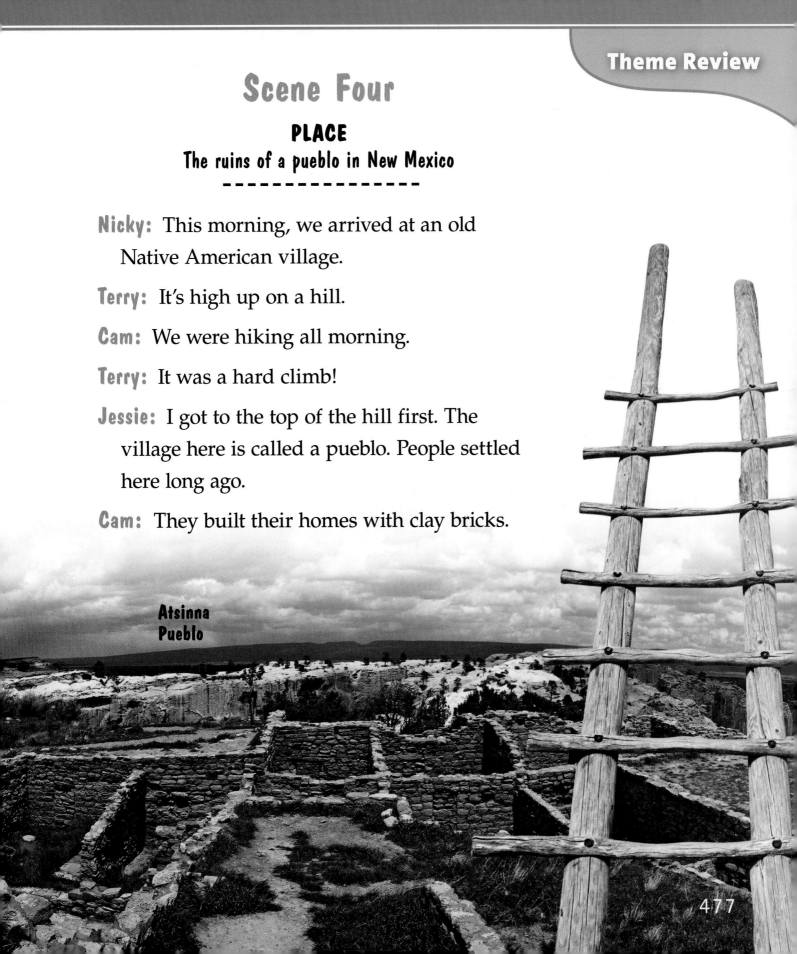

Scene Four

PLACE
The ruins of a pueblo in New Mexico

- - - - - - - - - - - - - - - - -

Nicky: This morning, we arrived at an old Native American village.

Terry: It's high up on a hill.

Cam: We were hiking all morning.

Terry: It was a hard climb!

Jessie: I got to the top of the hill first. The village here is called a pueblo. People settled here long ago.

Cam: They built their homes with clay bricks.

Atsinna
Pueblo

477

Mom: Then they left. For many years, no one lived here. Later, people found the ruins of the village.

Dad: After the discovery, scientists started studying the ruins. They found broken pots and worn stones. These helped them understand how the people cooked and what they ate long ago.

Jessie: No one knows exactly why the people who once lived here left, but scientists are still trying to find out.

Terry: I'd like to stay here longer.

ruins

Scene Five

PLACE
The San Gabriel Mountains in California

- - - - - - - - - - - - - - - - -

Dad: Today we're in the San Gabriel Mountains in California.

Mom: This is our last stop before we reach the Pacific Ocean.

Cam: We drove all day to get here. We finally stopped when the sun started to set behind these majestic mountains.

Nicky: It was impressive.

Mom: Tomorrow morning, we're going to ride mountain bikes up one of the mountains.

Jessie: I'll be the first one to the top!

Terry: I don't think so!

Cam: You'll both have to beat me!

Fluency Tip

For smooth reading, break long sentences into groups of words that go together.

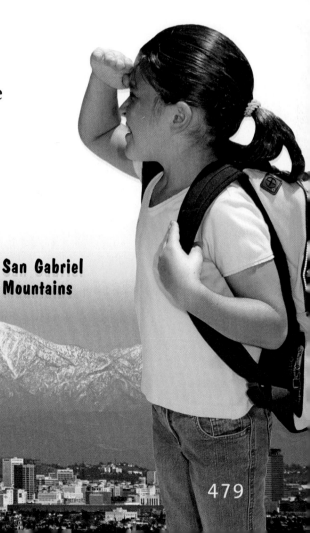

San Gabriel
Mountains

479

Scene Six

PLACE
The beach at Santa Monica, California

Cam: We've made it to the California coast! Aunt Fran's house is just a few minutes away.

Nicky: It took us fourteen days to get here! We're all feeling upbeat.

Terry: We're looking at the largest ocean in the world!

Cam: We're going to go swimming now.

Jessie: I'm going surfing!

Nicky: I hope the water is warm. I've heard that the water in the Pacific Ocean can be very cold!

Mom: Thanks for taking this video tour of the United States with us.

Dad: Last one in the water is a rotten egg!

Everyone: Here we go—good-bye!

Fluency Tip

Exclamation points let you know that someone is excited.

lifeguard station

481

COMPREHENSION STRATEGIES
Review

Reading Functional Text

Bridge to Reading for Information

Functional text is writing that people read every day. It is found on a cereal box, in the newspaper, and even in a phone book. Functional text helps people answer questions and complete tasks.

Read the notes on page 483 for kinds of functional text.

Review the Focus Strategies

Use the strategies you learned in this theme to help you read functional text.

Use Graphic Organizers
Graphic organizers can help you organize information you read.

Be Water Safe

Monitor Comprehension—Reread
If something you are reading does not make sense, reread it.

Use comprehension strategies as you read "Summer Safety" on pages 484–485.

INSTRUCTIONS
Instructions tell you how to do something.

SUMMER SAFETY

Be Wheel Safe

If you ride a bike, ride a scooter, or use in-line skates, be wheel safe. The most serious way kids get hurt while on wheels is by hitting their heads. So always wear a helmet when you are playing on wheels. When you ride scooters and use in-line skates, always wear wrist guards, kneepads, and elbow pads.

What's the Right Way to Wear a Helmet?

- A helmet should be straight on the head, just above the eyebrows.
- A helmet should fit snugly.
- The chin strap should be snug but not too tight.
- The rear straps go behind the ears. The front straps should run up and down.

Be Water Safe

One way to beat the summer heat is by swimming in a cool pool. To stay safe when you swim, you need to follow the water-safety rules. Be water safe by swimming only when a grown-up is nearby. You should always swim with a buddy.

Pool Safety Rules

- Do not run.
- Never play rough.
- Always jump in feet first.

LISTS
A list tells you things to remember about a topic.

SIGNS
A sign gives information that is quick and easy to read.

Apply the Strategies Read these pages about summer safety. As you read, stop and think about how you are using comprehension strategies.

SUMMER SAFETY

Be Wheel Safe

If you ride a bike, ride a scooter, or use in-line skates, be wheel safe. The most serious way kids get hurt while on wheels is by hitting their heads. So always wear a helmet when you are playing on wheels. When you ride scooters and use in-line skates, always wear wrist guards, kneepads, and elbow pads.

What's the Right Way to Wear a Helmet?

- A helmet should be straight on the head, just above the eyebrows.
- A helmet should fit snugly.
- The chin strap should be snug but not too tight.
- The rear straps go behind the ears. The front straps should run up and down.

Stop and Think

How would using a graphic organizer help you read instructions? How does rereading help you?

Be Water Safe

One way to beat the summer heat is by swimming in a cool pool. To stay safe when you swim, you need to follow the water-safety rules. Be water safe by swimming only when a grown-up is nearby. You should always swim with a buddy.

Pool Safety Rules

- Do not run.
- Never play rough.
- Always jump in feet first.

Using the Glossary

Get to Know It!

The **Glossary** gives the meaning of a word as it is used in the *Student Edition*. It also gives an example sentence that shows how to use the word. The words in the **Glossary** are in ABC order, also called alphabetical order.

Learn to Use It!

If you want to find *carefree* in the **Glossary**, you should first find the **C** words. **C** is near the beginning of the alphabet, so the **C** words are near the beginning of the **Glossary**. Then you can use the guide words at the top of the page to help you find the entry word *carefree*. It is on page 488.

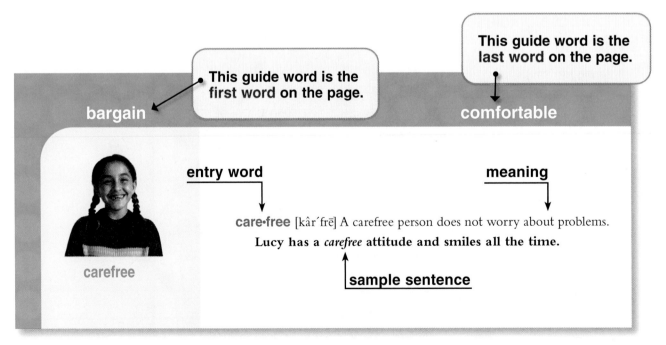

This guide word is the first word on the page.

This guide word is the last word on the page.

bargain   comfortable

entry word   meaning

care·free [kâr´frē] A carefree person does not worry about problems.
Lucy has a *carefree* attitude and smiles all the time.

sample sentence

carefree

A

ac·com·plish [ə·kom′plish] When you accomplish a task, you have completed it with good results. **I always feel good when I *accomplish* a goal.**

ac·cu·ra·cy [ak′yər·ə·sē] When you do something with accuracy, you do it without any mistakes. **Our teacher complimented Madison on her *accuracy* because she read the poem without making one mistake.**

ac·cu·rate·ly [ak′yər·it·lē] When you do something without making any mistakes, you have done it accurately. **Her math test was done *accurately*.**

ad·mit [ad·mit′] When you admit something, you agree that it is true, even though you might not want to. **I *admit* that I was wrong.**

ar·e·a [âr′ē·ə] An area is an open space or a part of a place. **The *area* beside the chalkboard is dusty.**

at·tack [ə·tak′] If you attack something, you use great force to try to cause it harm. **The cats will *attack* anything that moves.**

at·tend [ə·tend′] If you attend an event, you go to it. **Keisha will *attend* the dance tomorrow night.**

a·ward [ə·wôrd′] When you do something that others think is very good, you may receive a prize or an award. **Heather got an *award* for keeping her desk clean.**

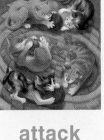

attack

award

B

bare·ly [bâr′lē] When you can barely do something, you almost can't do it at all. **Maria could *barely* see out of the window.**

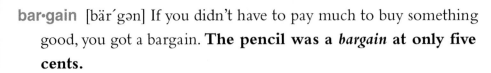

bar·gain [bär´gən] If you didn't have to pay much to buy something good, you got a bargain. **The pencil was a *bargain* at only five cents.**

be·yond [bi·yond´] Something that is beyond something else is farther away. ***Beyond* the fence was a field with cows.**

blend·ed [blend´əd] When things are blended, they are mixed together so that you can't tell there are separate parts. **Melissa *blended* yellow and blue to make green.**

boost [boōst] If you give someone a boost, you help lift him or her up to reach something. **He will need a *boost* to reach the water fountain.**

budge [buj] If you budge something, you move it just a little. **I can't seem to *budge* this heavy box.**

carefree

care·free [kâr´frē] A carefree person does not worry about problems. **Lucy has a *carefree* attitude and smiles all the time.**

care·ful·ly [kâr´fəl·lē] When you do something carefully, you pay close attention to what you are doing so that you don't make a mistake. **Grandma unwraps presents *carefully* so that she doesn't rip the paper.**

cel·e·brate [sel´ə·brāt] If you are happy about something, you may have a party to celebrate. **He likes to *celebrate* his birthday with friends.**

celebrate

col·lec·tion [kə·lek´shən] When you have a collection, you have a group of things that are kept together. **Jane has a large doll *collection*.**

com·fort·a·ble [kum´fər·tə·bəl] When you are comfortable, you feel good just as you are. **I feel *comfortable* wearing this soft jacket.**

com·mit·tee [kə·mit´ē] When you are on a committee, you work with a group of people on a project or for a special reason. **A *committee* will decide who wins the art contest.**

com·mon [kom´ən] If something is common, there is a lot of it or it happens often. **It is *common* to see crabs running on the beach.**

con·cen·trate [kon´sən·trāt] When you concentrate, you put all of your attention on one thing. **You must *concentrate* to solve the puzzle.**

co·zy [kō´zē] If a place is cozy, it makes you feel warm, happy, and comfortable. **The kitten curls up in its *cozy* little cat bed.**

cra·dled [krād´(ə)ld] If you cradle something, you hold it closely as if you were taking care of it. **Laura *cradled* her guinea pig.**

cre·ate [krē·āt´] When you create, you use your imagination to make something new. **He can *create* such funny stories.**

cre·a·tive [krē·ā´tiv] If you are creative, you use new or different ideas to make or do something. **Dawn is very *creative* in the way she uses colors in her art.**

crop [krop] A large planting of one kind of plant is a crop. **We grew a large *crop* of pumpkins this year.**

crowd [kroud] When people or animals gather in large numbers, they crowd together. **The children began to *crowd* around the artist as he painted a picture.**

crum·pled [krum´pəld] If you crumple something, you gently crush it or bunch it up. **The writer *crumpled* his story and threw it in the trash.**

cradled

creative

crop

D

de·lay [di·lā´] If you delay something, you keep it from happening as soon as it should. **Line up quickly so that we will not *delay* our lunch.**

de·liv·ered [di·liv´ərd] If you deliver something, you take it from one place and bring it to another. **They *delivered* the pizza so quickly!**

dis·ap·pear [dis·ə·pir´] When something disappears, you can't see it anymore. **Watch the bubbles *disappear* in the air!**

dis·cov·er·y [dis·kuv´ər·ē] When you learn something or find something for the first time, you make a discovery. **A way to keep people from getting colds would be an important *discovery*.**

dis·tance [dis´təns] Distance is how far away something is. **The park was at a great *distance* from Li's house.**

delivered

E

earn [ûrn] When you earn, you get money or some other kind of reward for doing something. **Jimmy will rake leaves to *earn* money for a new baseball mitt.**

en·chant·ing [in·chant´ing] If you think someone or something is enchanting, you think that person or thing is likeable and enjoyable. **The princess was *enchanting* when she smiled.**

en·ter·tain [en·tər·tān´] When you entertain an audience, you do something, such as acting or singing, that you think people will enjoy. **We like to *entertain* our friends with puppet shows.**

en·tire [in·tīr´] An entire thing is all of that thing. **Pedro's *entire* room was clean.**

entertain

ex·cept [ik·sept´] When you talk about every thing except one, you mean all but that one. **Every grade *except* kindergarten can take part in the spelling bee.**

ex·changed [iks·chānjd´] When you exchanged things, you gave something to someone and you got something else in return. **She *exchanged* phone numbers with Sandy so that they could call each other after school.**

ex·per·i·ments [ik·sper´ə·mənts] Experiments are tests to try out an idea or to find out if something is true. **Paul's *experiments* proved that cats do not enjoy baths but do enjoy toys.**

ex·pres·sion [ik·spresh´ən] If you use expression when you speak, you use your voice, your face, or your body to add meaning to what you say. Reading aloud with expression is using your voice to match the action of the story and the characters' feelings. **The *expression* in the storyteller's face and voice made it clear that the character was delighted.**

expression

ex·treme·ly [ik·strēm´lē] Something that is extremely a certain way is very much that way. **The line for the movie was *extremely* long and moved slowly.**

fan·tas·tic [fan·tas´tik] If something is fantastic, it is wonderful. **The field trip to the zoo was *fantastic!***

fea·si·ble [fē´zə·bəl] If something is feasible, it can be done. **It is *feasible* that we can get there on time if we hurry.**

fic·tion [fik´shən] Fiction is writing that tells a story with characters, setting, and plot. **Jarod knew that the book was *fiction* because one of the characters was a talking dog.**

fra·grant [frā´grənt] Something that is fragrant has a pleasing, sweet smell. **I can smell the *fragrant* flowers outside the window.**

fragrant

grand

hilarious

G

gen·re [zhän´rə] Genre is writing style. **Bobby likes detective stories, so he reads books in the mystery *genre*.**

gen·tly [jen´tlē] If you do something gently, you do it in a way that is careful and kind. **Sal petted the newborn colt very *gently*.**

grand [grand] If something is grand, it is important and wonderful. **We saw a *grand* parade on the Fourth of July.**

grunt·ed [grunt´əd] If you grunted, you made a small, deep sound in your throat. **The strong man *grunted* when he lifted the weights.**

H

hi·lar·i·ous [hi·lâr´ē·əs] When you think something is hilarious, you think it is very, very funny. **It was *hilarious* when the giraffe stuck out its tongue!**

his·tor·i·cal [his·tôr´ə·kəl] Something that is historical is part of history. **There were many *historical* items in the museum.**

host [hōst] The host of a program introduces the guests and talks with them. **Ms. Miller will be the *host* for our guest speakers.**

I

im·pres·sive [im·pres´iv] When you think something is impressive, you think it is very, very good. **Lisa's speech was *impressive*.**

in·stead [in·sted´] When you do one thing instead of a second thing, you do it in place of the second thing. **Use a pen, *instead* of a pencil, to write the letter.**

in·to·na·tion [in´tō·nā´shən] Intonation is the rise and fall of your voice as you read aloud. **The *intonation* of her voice changed when she read the adventure story.**

last [last] Something that will last will be able to be used for a long time. **The new steel bridge will *last* a very long time.**

lit·er·a·ture [lit´ər·ə·chər] Stories and poems are kinds of literature. **That poem is my favorite piece of *literature*.**

ma·jes·tic [mə·jes´tik] If something is majestic, it seems as important and grand as a king or a queen. **The *majestic* mountain had a cap of white snow.**

majestic

non·fic·tion [non´fik´shən] Nonfiction is writing that gives information about a topic. **Juan wanted to learn about dinosaurs, so he checked out a *nonfiction* book.**

no·ticed [nō´tist] If you noticed something, you observed it carefully. **All of us *noticed* how well the music teacher sang.**

P

pat·tern [pat´ərn] When you see a design in something, you are seeing a pattern. **The lighthouse had a *pattern* of stripes.**

peer [pir] If you peer, you look closely at something. **The principal would *peer* through the door to see why we were noisy.** *Another meaning*—A person who is equal to you in age or can do something as well as you is your peer. **Jill was placed on a soccer team with her *peers* from the second grade.**

pattern

per·form·ance [pər·fôr´məns] When you sing, dance, or act in front of an audience, you are giving a performance. **Jenny's dance** *performance* **was very good.**

per·son·al·i·ties [pûr·sən·al´ə·tēz] People's personalities are made up of all the ways they act, think, and feel that make them special. **All of the performers had such friendly** *personalities***!**

phras·ing [frāz´ing] Phrasing is grouping words that go together when you read aloud. **When Elsa learned to use** *phrasing***, she was able to read smoothly.**

plead·ed [plēd´əd] If you plead, you beg someone for something. **Frank's cousin** *pleaded* **to be allowed to go with us.**

pro·vide [prə·vīd´] When you provide something, you give it to someone. **Please** *provide* **me with an address so I can mail the letter.**

punc·tu·a·tion [pungk·chōō·ā´shən] Punctuation marks are used in sentences to show meaning to the reader. **Some** *punctuation* **marks, such as periods, go at the end of a sentence.**

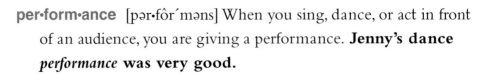

rag·ged·y [rag´id·ē] When something is raggedy, it looks rough and torn at the edges, like a rag. **Our clothes looked** *raggedy* **after we had been camping for two weeks.**

rare [râr] If something is rare, it is not found or seen very often. **I found a** *rare* **Spanish coin at the beach.** *Another meaning*—If you like meat that has not been cooked very long, you like it rare. **My uncle orders steak cooked** *rare,* **but I like mine well done.**

read·ing rate [rē´ding rāt] Your reading rate is the speed at which you can read correctly and also understand what you are reading. **As Josh read more books, his** *reading rate* **became faster.**

performance

rare

re·lieved [ri·lēvd´] If you are relieved, you feel happy because some kind of worry is gone. **I was *relieved* to find my books where I had left them.**

re·plied [ri·plīd´] When you answered someone's question, you replied. **John always *replied* politely to his uncle.**

re·port [ri·pôrt´] When you make a report, you tell what you have learned or found out. **Tim's *report* was about bears.**

re·sponds [ri·spondz´] If someone responds to a question, he or she is giving an answer. **Celeste *responds* often to questions in class.**

responds

re·view [ri·vyoo´] If you say or write what you think about a play, a book, or a movie, you are giving a review. **The *review* in the newspaper said that this movie was very good.**

risk [risk] If you take a risk, you take a chance of harm or a bad result. **You take a *risk* of falling if you run in the rain.**

 S

scampering

scam·per·ing [skam´pər·ing] If you were scampering, you were running in a playful way. **It's fun to watch the kittens *scampering* and playing in the backyard.**

screech·ing [skrēch´ing] If you hear a screeching noise, you hear a loud, high sound that can hurt your ears. **The roller coaster made a *screeching* sound when it went around the curve.**

screeching

seal [sēl] If you seal something, you close it up tightly. ***Seal* the box before you mail it.** *Another meaning*—A seal is an animal with fins that spends time both in the water and on land. **A *seal* can swim in the water better than it can walk on land.**

sep·a·rat·ed [sep´ə·rāt·əd] If you separated things, you sorted them into groups. **Tasha *separated* the red blocks from the blue blocks.**

serve

statue

se·ri·ous [sir´ē·əs] When something is serious, it is important and not at all funny. **A fire alarm is a *serious* matter.**

serve [sûrve] When you serve people, you bring them food and drinks. ***Serve* breakfast to your mother.**

set·tled [set´əld] If something settled, it moved slowly until it came to rest. **The soil *settled* to the bottom of the pail of water.**

sipped [sipt] If you sipped, you took a very small drink of something. **Rachel *sipped* the soda slowly so that she would not get hiccups.**

sleuths [slo͞oths] Sleuths are people who try to solve crimes or mysteries. **Detectives are *sleuths* who work to solve crimes.**

smoth·ered [smuth´ərd] If you smother something, you cover it completely so that it has no air. **We *smothered* the campfire with sand to put out the flames.**

spare [spâr] If you have spare time, money, or space, you have extra that you do not need. **Do you have some *spare* paper that I could use?**

spoiled [spoild] If you spoiled something, you damaged or ruined it. **The painting was *spoiled* when Adam folded it while it was still wet.**

stat·ue [stach´o͞o] A statue is a work of art, often showing a person, that can be seen from all sides. It may be made of wood, stone, bronze, or some other hard material. **I saw a *statue* of Abraham Lincoln.**

stomped [stompt] If you stomped, you used your feet to make heavy, pounding steps. **Stan *stomped* his feet on the mat to get the dirt off his shoes.**

sup·plies [sə·plīz´] Supplies are the materials and equipment needed to do a job. **Bring *supplies* such as glue and ribbon for the project.**

syl·la·ble [sil´ə·bəl] A syllable is the smallest part of a word that includes a vowel sound. ***Picnic* is a word that includes two *syllables*.**

T
---

thrilled [thrild] If something thrilled you, it made you feel excited and happy. **I was *thrilled* to jump into the swimming pool on such a hot day!**

U
---

up·beat [up´bēt] If you are upbeat, you are cheerful. **No matter what happens, Rob is always *upbeat* about it.**

V
---

vol·ume [vol´yo͞om] When you change the volume on a TV or a radio, you change how loud or soft the sound is. **The *volume* of the radio was too low for me to hear.**

W
---

wit·ty [wit´ē] If you are witty, you say things in a clever and funny way. **My uncle is *witty* and tells good jokes.**

supplies

upbeat

Index of Titles and Authors

Page numbers in green refer to biographical information.

Ada, Alma Flor, 386, 434, 462

"Ah, Music!," 98

Aliki, 98, 111

"Annie's Gifts," 58

"Be Sun Safe," 464

"Bee, The," 244

"Beyond Old MacDonald," 234

Brown, Monica, 368, 385

"California Bee Business," 274

Campoy, F. Isabel, 386

"Chair For My Mother, A," 166

"Chimp Computer Whiz," 298

"Come, My Little Children, Here Are Songs for You," 112

Crewe, Sabrina, 244, 273

"Cross-Country Vacation," 470

Egan, Tim, 208, 233

Firestone, Mary, 192

"Gabriela Mistral: A Poet's Life In Photos," 386

Gans, Roma, 398, 423

Haberle, Susan E., 354

Hennessey, Gail Skroback, 136

Hoce, Charley, 234

"Interview With California Author Pam Muñoz Ryan," 44

Katz, Susan, 88

"Let's Go Rock Collecting," 398

"Life of George Washington Carver, The," 122

"Lizard and the Sun, The," 434

Lynch, Tom, 316

Medearis, Angela Shelf, 58, 87

"Mr. Putter and Tabby Write the Book," 22

"My Name Is Gabriela," 368

"North America," 154

"Nutty Facts About Peanuts," 136

Park, Frances and Ginger, 328, 352

"Pebbles," 424

Rylant, Cynthia, 22, 43

"Sarah Enters a Painting," 88

"Saving Money," 192

"Serious Farm," 208

Simon, Charnan, 284, 297

"South Korea," 354

Stevens, Joli K., 122

Stevenson, Robert Louis, 112

"Summer Safety," 482

"Time for Patience, A," 316

"Town Hall," 304

"Watching in the Wild," 284

"What's My Job?," 142

"Where on Earth Is My Bagel?," 328

Williams, Vera B., 166, 191

Worth, Valerie, 424

CALIFORNIA READING

English-Language Arts Content Standards

 **READING**

1.0 **Word Analysis, Fluency, and Systematic Vocabulary Development**
Students understand the basic features of reading. They select letter patterns and know how to translate them into spoken language by using phonics, syllabication, and word parts. They apply this knowledge to achieve fluent oral and silent reading.

Decoding and Word Recognition

1.1 Recognize and use knowledge of spelling patterns (e.g., diphthongs, special vowel spellings) when reading.

1.2 Apply knowledge of basic syllabication rules when reading (e.g., vowel-consonant-vowel = *su/per*; vowel-consonant/consonant-vowel = *sup/per*).

1.3 Decode two-syllable nonsense words and regular multisyllable words.

1.4 Recognize common abbreviations (e.g., *Jan., Sun., Mr., St.*).

1.5 Identify and correctly use regular plurals (e.g., *-s, -es, -ies*) and irregular plurals (e.g., *fly/flies, wife/wives*).

1.6 Read aloud fluently and accurately and with appropriate intonation and expression.

Vocabulary and Concept Development

1.7 Understand and explain common antonyms and synonyms.

1.8 Use knowledge of individual words in unknown compound words to predict their meaning.

1.9 Know the meaning of simple prefixes and suffixes (e.g., *over-*, *un-*, *-ing*, *-ly*).

1.10 Identify simple multiple-meaning words.

2.0 **Reading Comprehension**
Students read and understand grade-level-appropriate material. They draw upon a variety of comprehension strategies as needed (e.g., generating and responding to essential questions, making predictions, comparing information from several sources). The selections in *Recommended Readings in Literature, Kindergarten Through Grade Eight* illustrate the quality and complexity of the materials to be read by students. In addition to their regular school reading, by grade four, students read one-half million words annually, including a good representation of grade-level-appropriate narrative and expository text (e.g., classic and contemporary

literature, magazines, newspapers, online information). In grade two, students continue to make progress toward this goal.

Structural Features of Informational Materials

2.1   Use titles, tables of contents, and chapter headings to locate information in expository text.

Comprehension and Analysis of Grade-Level-Appropriate Text

2.2   State the purpose in reading (i.e., tell what information is sought).

2.3   Use knowledge of the author's purpose(s) to comprehend informational text.

2.4   Ask clarifying questions about essential textual elements of exposition (e.g., *why, what if, how*).

2.5   Restate facts and details in the text to clarify and organize ideas.

2.6   Recognize cause-and-effect relationships in a text.

2.7   Interpret information from diagrams, charts, and graphs.

2.8   Follow two-step written instructions.

3.0 Literary Response and Analysis

Students read and respond to a wide variety of significant works of children's literature. They distinguish between the structural features of the text and the literary terms or elements (e.g., theme, plot, setting, characters). The selections in *Recommended Readings in Literature, Kindergarten Through Grade Eight* illustrate the quality and complexity of the materials to be read by students.

Narrative Analysis of Grade-Level-Appropriate Text

3.1 Compare and contrast plots, settings, and characters presented by different authors.

3.2 Generate alternative endings to plots and identify the reason or reasons for, and the impact of, the alternatives.

3.3 Compare and contrast different versions of the same stories that reflect different cultures.

3.4 Identify the use of rhythm, rhyme, and alliteration in poetry.

 **WRITING**

1.0 Writing Strategies

Students write clear and coherent sentences and paragraphs that develop a central idea. Their writing shows they consider the audience and purpose.

Students progress through the stages of the writing process (e.g., prewriting, drafting, revising, editing successive versions).

Organization and Focus

1.1 Group related ideas and maintain a consistent focus.

Penmanship

1.2 Create readable documents with legible handwriting.

Research

1.3 Understand the purposes of various reference materials (e.g., dictionary, thesaurus, atlas).

Evaluation and Revision

1.4 Revise original drafts to improve sequence and provide more descriptive detail.

2.0 **Writing Applications (Genres and Their Characteristics)**
Students write compositions that describe and explain familiar objects, events, and experiences. Student writing demonstrates a command of standard American English and the drafting, research, and organizational strategies outlined in Writing Standard 1.0.

Using the writing strategies of grade two outlined in Writing Standard 1.0, students:

2.1 Write brief narratives based on their experiences:

    a. Move through a logical sequence of events.

    b. Describe the setting, characters, objects, and events in detail.

2.2 Write a friendly letter complete with the date, salutation, body, closing, and signature.

 WRITTEN AND ORAL ENGLISH LANGUAGE CONVENTIONS

The standards for written and oral English language conventions have been placed between those for writing and for listening and speaking because these conventions are essential to both sets of skills.

1.0 **Written and Oral English Language Conventions**
Students write and speak with a command of standard English conventions appropriate to this grade level.

Sentence Structure

1.1 Distinguish between complete and incomplete sentences.

1.2 Recognize and use the correct word order in written sentences.

Grammar

1.3   Identify and correctly use various parts of speech, including nouns and verbs, in writing and speaking.

Punctuation

1.4   Use commas in the greeting and closure of a letter and with dates and items in a series.

1.5   Use quotation marks correctly.

Capitalization

1.6   Capitalize all proper nouns, words at the beginning of sentences and greetings, months and days of the week, and titles and initials of people.

Spelling

1.7   Spell frequently used, irregular words correctly (e.g., *was, were, says, said, who, what, why*).

1.8   Spell basic short-vowel, long-vowel, *r*-controlled, and consonant-blend patterns correctly.

1.0 Listening and Speaking Strategies

Students listen critically and respond appropriately to oral communication. They speak in a manner that guides the listener to understand important ideas by using proper phrasing, pitch, and modulation.

Comprehension

1.1 Determine the purpose or purposes of listening (e.g., to obtain information, to solve problems, for enjoyment).

1.2 Ask for clarification and explanation of stories and ideas.

1.3 Paraphrase information that has been shared orally by others.

1.4 Give and follow three- and four-step oral directions.

Organization and Delivery of Oral Communication

1.5 Organize presentations to maintain a clear focus.

1.6 Speak clearly and at an appropriate pace for the type of communication (e.g., informal discussion, report to class).

1.7 Recount experiences in a logical sequence.

1.8   Retell stories, including characters, setting, and plot.

1.9   Report on a topic with supportive facts and details.

2.0   **Speaking Applications (Genres and Their Characteristics)**
Students deliver brief recitations and oral presentations about familiar experiences or interests that are organized around a coherent thesis statement. Student speaking demonstrates a command of standard American English and the organizational and delivery strategies outlined in Listening and Speaking Standard 1.0.

Using the speaking strategies of grade two outlined in Listening and Speaking Standard 1.0, students:

2.1   Recount experiences or present stories:

  a. Move through a logical sequence of events.

  b. Describe story elements (e.g., characters, plot, setting).

2.2   Report on a topic with facts and details, drawing from several sources of information.

Acknowledgments

For permission to reprint copyrighted material, grateful acknowledgment is made to the following sources:

Boyds Mills Press, Inc.: "Mischievous Goat," "Farm Family," and "When My Cow Goes Dancing" from *Beyond Old MacDonald: Funny Poems from Down on the Farm* by Charley Hoce, illustrated by Eugenie Fernandes. Text copyright © 2005 by Charley Hoce; illustrations copyright © 2005 by Eugenie Fernandes. Published by Wordsong, an imprint of Boyds Mills Press.

Capstone Press: From *Saving Money* by Mary Firestone. Text copyright © 2005 by Capstone Press. From *South Korea* by Susan E. Haberle, map by Nancy Steers. Text and map copyright © 2005 by Capstone Press.

Children's Better Health Institute, Indianapolis, IN: From "Be Sun Safe" by Daniel Lee in *U.S. Kids* Magazine, July/August 2004. Text copyright © 2004 by Children's Better Health Institute, Benjamin Franklin Literary & Medical Society, Inc.

The Cricket Magazine Group, a division of Carus Publishing Company: From "Chimp Computer Whiz" in *Ask* Magazine, March 2006. Text © 2006 by Carus Publishing Company.

Farrar, Straus and Giroux, LLC: "Pebbles" from *All the Small Poems and Fourteen More* by Valerie Worth. Text copyright © 1987, 1994 by Valerie Worth.

Harcourt, Inc.: *Mr. Putter & Tabby Write the Book* by Cynthia Rylant, illustrated by Arthur Howard. Text copyright © 2004 by Cynthia Rylant; illustrations copyright © 2004 by Arthur Howard.

HarperCollins Publishers: From *Ah, Music!* by Aliki. Copyright © 2003 by Aliki Brandenberg. *Let's Go Rock Collecting* by Roma Gans, illustrated by Holly Keller. Text copyright © 1984, 1997 by Roma Gans; illustrations copyright © 1997 by Holly Keller. *A Chair for My Mother* by Vera B. Williams. Copyright © 1982 by Vera B. Williams.

Heinemann-Raintree, Chicago, IL: From *The Bee* by Sabrina Crewe, illustrated by Stuart Lafford. Text and illustrations copyright © 1997 by Steck-Vaughn Company.

Houghton Mifflin Company: *Serious Farm* by Tim Egan. Copyright © 2003 by Tim Egan.

Just Us Books, Inc.: Annie's Gifts by Angela Shelf Medearis, illustrated by Anna Rich. Text copyright 1994 by Angela Shelf Medearis; illustrations copyright 1994 by Anna Rich.

Lee & Low Books, Inc., New York, NY 10016: Where on Earth Is My Bagel? by Frances Park and Ginger Park, illustrated by Grace Lin. Text copyright © 2001 by Frances Park and Ginger Park; illustrations copyright © 2001 by Grace Lin.

National Wildlife Federation®: From "Nutty Facts About Peanuts" by Gail Skroback Hennessey in *Ranger Rick®* Magazine, January 2004. Text copyright 2004 by the National Wildlife Federation®.

National Wildlife Federation® and Danielle Jones: Illustrations by Danielle Jones from "Nutty Facts About Peanuts" by Gail Skroback Hennessey in *Ranger Rick®* Magazine, January 2004. Illustrations © 2004 by Danielle Jones.

Northland Publishing, Flagstaff, AZ 86002: My Name Is Gabriela/Me llamo Gabriela by Monica Brown, illustrated by John Parra. Text copyright © 2005 by Monica Brown; illustrations copyright © 2005 by John Parra, Vicki Prentice Associates, Inc. NYC.

Random House Children's Books, a division of Random House, Inc., New York, NY: The Lizard and the Sun/La Lagartija y el Sol by Alma Flor Ada, illustrated by Felipe Dávalos. Text copyright © 1997 by Alma Flor Ada; illustrations copyright © 1997 by Felipe Dávalos.

Charnan Simon: "Watching in the Wild" by Charnan Simon. Text copyright 2004 by Charnan Simon. Originally published in *Click* Magazine, January 2004.

Simon & Schuster Books for Young Readers, an imprint of Simon & Schuster Children's Publishing Division: "Sarah Enters a Painting" from *Mrs. Brown on Exhibit and Other Museum Poems* by Susan Katz, illustrated by R. W. Alley. Text copyright © 2002 by Susan Katz; illustrations copyright © 2002 by R. W. Alley.

Viking Children's Books, A Division of Penguin Young Readers Group, A Member of Penguin Group (USA) Inc., 345 Hudson Street, New York, NY 10014: "A Time for Patience" from *Fables from Aesop*, retold and illustrated by Tom Lynch. Copyright © 2000 by Tom Lynch.

Weekly Reader Corporation: From "Be Wheel Safe" and "Be Water Safe" (Retitled: "Summer Safety") in *Weekly Reader* Magazine, Edition 2, May 2, 2003. Text published and copyrighted by Weekly Reader Corporation.

Photo Credits

Placement Key; (t) top; (b) bottom; (l) left; (r) right; (c) center; (bg) background; (fg) foreground; (i) inset

19 (tr) Klaus Hackenberg/zefa/Corbis; 94 (c)Robert Llewellyn/Corbis; 94 (cr) Virgo/zefa/Corbis; 95 (tl) Erin Patrice O'Brien/Getty Images; 95 (c)Steve Campbell/Getty Images; 119 (tr) The Granger Collection, New York; 164 (bl) From PhotoDisc's the Object's Series; 275; (tr) Richard Bickel/Corbis; 275 (l) Silver Image; 282 (tr) Shutterstock; 282 (t) Shutterstock; 283 (tr) Paul Kennedy / LPI; 324 (br) Rita Maas/Dynamic Graphics/Jupiterimages; 365 (b) Kevin Cozad/O'Brien Productions/Corbis; 395 (cl) Brand X/SuperStock; 395 (bl) Ryan McVay/Taxi/Getty Images; 464 (bl) Danny Lee.

All other photos © Harcourt School Publishers. Harcourt photos provided by Harcourt Index, Harcourt IPR, and Harcourt Photographers: Weronica Ankarorn, Eric Camden, Doug DuKane, Ken Kinsie, April Riehm and Steve Williams.

Illustration Credits

Cover Art; Laura and Eric Ovresat, Artlab, Inc.

H.S.P. CALIFORNIA EXCURSIONS

It takes you there!